@Copyright 2020 By Lauren Neales **All Rights reserved**

The Declaration of Principles accepted and supported by the American Bar Association Committee and the Publishers and Associations Committee.

Not the least bit is permissible for any piece of this report to be replicated,copied or transmitted in either electronic methods or the group.The recording of this distribution is carefully refused, and any capacity in this report is not allowed unless the distributor has composed the authorization. All rights.

The data in this is conveyed,to be truthful and predictable,inasmuch as any danger, to absent mind or something else,is a single and articulate duty of a beneficiary peruser through use or maltreatment of any methods, procedures, or bearings embedded within it.No lawful obligation or default shall be made against the distributor for any reparation,damage,or money misfortune due to the information in this,either directly or implicitly.

Any copyrights not held by the seller are asserted by individual authors.

The data in this document is only available for educational purposes and is all-inclusive.The data are entered without a contract or confirmation of assurance.

The marks used shall be without consent, and the mark shall be distributed without the consent or support of the proprietor.All trademarks and trademarks in this book are for explanation only and are clearly held by owners who are not associated with the record.

CONTENTS

The Complete Guide to a Plant-Based Diet..... 4
- What Is a Plant-Based Diet And Why Should You Try It? 4
- Your Plant-Based Questions, Answered. 5
- 10 Simple Plant-Based Recipes To Get You Started 6

Best Instant Pot Cookbooks & Plant-Based Diet............... 9

Breakfast 10
- Cinnamon Apple Porridge............... 10
- Peanut Butter & Chocolate Steel Cut Oats 11
- Fruity Quinoa & Granola Bowls 12
- Oats With Milk And Blueberry 13
- Kale And Sweet Potato Mini Quiche 14
- Poblano-Sweet Potato Hash 15
- Tempeh Sausage 16
- Cinnamon Apple Porridge............... 17
- Peanut Butter & Chocolate Steel Cut Oats 18
- Fruity Quinoa & Granola Bowls 19
- Healthy-Yet-Tasty Oats 20
- Kale & Sweet Potato Mini Quiche............ 21

Grains, Beans, and Legumes............... 22
- Green Chile Baked Beans 22
- Mexican Black Beans 23
- Refried Pinto Beans............... 24
- Red Beans & Rice............... 25
- Chickpea Basil Salad 26
- Green Chile Chickpeas............... 27
- Mediterranean Lentils 28
- Smoky Butternut Lentils............... 29
- Spicy Southwestern Lentils 30
- Cilantro Lime Brown Rice 31
- Biryani Rice 32

Spanish Rice 33
Potato And Green Bean Salad 34
Three Bean Delight............... 35
Green Chili Baked Beans 36
Mexican Black Beans 37
Refried Pinto Beans............... 38
Red Beans And Rice............... 39
Chickpea Basil Salad 40
Green Chili Chickpeas............... 41
Taco/Burrito Filling 42
Curried Lentils............... 43
Coconut Curry Tofu............... 44
Chipotle Chickpeas 45
Cinnamon Chickpeas 46

Soups, Stews & Chilis............... 47
- Veggie Noodle Soup............... 47
- Carrot Ginger Soup............... 48
- Creamy Tomato Basil Soup 49
- Cream Of Mushroom Soup 50
- Split Pea Soup 51
- Potato Leek Soup............... 52
- Cozy Wild Rice Soup 53
- Curried Squash Soup 54
- Smoky White Bean Soup 55
- Minestrone Soup 56
- Veggie Noodle Soup............... 57
- Carrot Ginger Soup............... 58
- Creamy Tomato Basil Soup 59
- Cream Of Mushroom Soup 60
- Split Pea Soup 61
- Potato Leek Soup............... 62
- Wild Rice Soup 63
- Curried Squash Soup 64

- Smoky White Bean Soup 65
- Minestrone Soup 66
- Lasagna Soup 67

Vegetable 68
- Mashed Potatoes 68
- Potato Salad 69
- Spicy Potato Bites With Avocado Dip 70
- Lemon-Dill Baby Potatoes 71
- Sweet Potato Breakfast Bowls 72
- Balsamic And Red Wine Mushrooms 73
- Ratatouille 74
- Spaghetti Squash Primavera 75
- Beet Marinara Sauce 76
- Butternut Squash And Pineapple 77
- Red Thai Curry Cauliflower 78
- Polenta & Kale 79
- Butternut Mac 'N' Cheese 80
- Sweet Potato & Black Bean Tacos 81
- Chickpea Kale Korma 82
- Deconstructed Cabbage Rolls 83
- Asian-Style Coconut Rice & Veggies 84
- Layered Mexican Casserole 85
- Moo Goo Gai Pan 86
- Vegetable Lasagna 87

Treats, Sweets & Desserts 89
- Bourbon Apple Crisp 89
- Vanilla Poached Pears With Caramel Sauce 90
- Fresh Fruit Compote 91
- Cinnamon-Vanilla Applesauce 92
- Bourbon Apple Crisp 93
- Poached Pears With Caramel Sauce 94
- Fresh Fruit Compote 95
- Cinnamon Coconut Rice Pudding 96
- Sticky Rice & Fresh Fruit 97
- Cherry Pie 98
- Mango Coconut Rice Pudding 99
- Tapioca Pudding 99

Appetizers, Starters & Sides 100
- Cowboy Caviar 100
- Beans With Jalapenos 101
- Candid Carrots 101
- Lemon Ginger Asparagus 102
- Steamed Artichokes 102
- Candied Carrots 103
- Anything-But-Basic Baked Potatoes 104
- Lemon Ginger Asparagus 105
- "Roasted" Garlic 106
- Steamed Artichokes 107

THE COMPLETE GUIDE TO A PLANT-BASED DIET

What Is a Plant-Based Diet And Why Should You Try It?

Plant-based or plant-forward eating patterns focus on foods primarily from plants. This includes not only fruits and vegetables, but also nuts, seeds, oils, whole grains, legumes, and beans. It doesn't mean that you are vegetarian or vegan and never eat meat or dairy. Rather, you are proportionately choosing more of your foods from plant sources.

What is the evidence that plant-based eating patterns are healthy? Much nutrition research has examined plant-based eating patterns such as the Mediterranean diet and a vegetarian diet. The Mediterranean diet has a foundation of plant-based foods; it also includes fish, poultry, eggs, cheese, and yogurt a few times a week, with meats and sweets less often.

Vegetarian diets have also been shown to support health, including a lower risk of developing coronary heart disease, high blood pressure, diabetes, and increased longevity.

Plant-based diets offer all the necessary protein, fats, carbohydrates, vitamins, and minerals for optimal health, and are often higher in fiber and phytonutrients. However, some vegans may need to add a supplement (specifically vitamin B12) to ensure they receive all the nutrients required.

Your Plant-Based Questions, Answered

We're sure you've got plenty of questions about the move to a whole-food, plant-based diet, and we're here to help.

How do I know if a whole-food, plant-based diet is for me?
You don't—until you try it! So many people who make the switch report feeling much better, having less fatigue, and losing weight, and otherwise enjoying a healthy lifestyle. We make the switch super easy with our extensive tools and resources. Once you get started, it'll be easier to keep going. As Dr. Craig McDougall says, "Once you have more energy, have lost some weight, or your stomach pain has disappeared, then it's easier to continue eating healthfully. One of the best motivators for people transitioning to plant-based eating comes from how great they feel and how much more they can do in their lives once they're feeling healthier."

Can I eat a plant-based diet on a budget?
Whole-food, plant-based eating is cheaper than you think. Fresh produce goes a long way, and whole grains, potatoes, and beans are some of the most affordable bulk foods you can buy. Create meals around these staple items and you'll definitely spend less than you do on a diet rich in meat and other animal products.

How can I eat whole-food, plant-based while traveling or away from home?
You will need to plan ahead a little, but it's pretty easy to find whole-food, plant-based meals on the go. You can usually find fruit and dishes made with pasta, rice, and potatoes wherever you are. With a little creativity and flexibility, you can also prepare some fantastic food to take with you.

How do I eat out on a plant-based diet?
Most restaurants are very accommodating of dietary needs, and you should be able to review their menu online. Scan the menu in advance to see if a restaurant offers vegan options, and you're already most of the way there. When you're unsure, simply call ahead, explain your preferences, and they will probably be able to accommodate you.

How do I make sure I get the nutrients I need?
Whole plant foods contain all the essential nutrients (with the exception of vitamin B12) we need. You can get some B12 from fortified foods such as plant-based milks and breakfast cereals, but the best source is a simple B12 supplement. (In fact, the U.S. Department of Health and Human Services recommends supplemental B12 for all adults over age 50 because as we age, many people lose the ability to absorb vitamin B12 from food sources.)

Is eating a whole-food, plant-based diet the same as being vegan?
While there are certainly some similarities between eating a whole-food, plant-based diet and being vegan, there are some differences as well. Vegans avoid all animal products or exploitation in food, clothing, shoes, or any other aspect of their lives. Vegans do not necessarily focus on whole plant foods; they may eat refined and processed foods, although many choose not to.

10 Simple Plant-Based Recipes To Get You Started

10 Plant-Based Snacks You Can Make in 5 Minutes. Fast, easy, delicious snacks for kids and big kids. As busy parents, it's easy to always feel like we're in a rush. Children are also growing fast and can seem hungry all the time. For both adults and children, it's easier to make bad choices when we're hungry, so keeping healthy, quick, and easy snacks nearby is important. Make sure you have a few simple items in your refrigerator or pantry so you'll be prepared when the snack monster hits. Here are ten go-to snacks to help keep your family going strong!

1.Big Bowl
Big Bowl is a combination of oats, whole-wheat cereals, raisins, walnuts and more. We love to pour our favorite plant-based milk on it (we rotate between rice, almond, and coconut milk) and then top it off with fresh fruit.

2.Veggies and Dip
Keep some pre-sliced veggies or baby carrots stored in your fridge. Serve with low-fat hummus, plant-based ranch, or any other dip that your family loves.

3. An Apple (or Any Other Fruit!) a Day
We all know what they say about apples, but don't forget about the simplest, purest form of energy out there: fresh fruit! Check out your local grocery store for in-season fruit and include it in your weekly shopping. To help you in grab-and-go situations, leave beautifully colored seasonal fruit like pears, peaches, nectarines, oranges, and apples out on top of the counter or in a nice bowl so you always see it. It's easy to grab and you will always have a snack on standby when you're in need!

4. Fruit Smoothies
Blend some frozen or fresh berries, a banana, and some plant-based milk for a quick and delicious snack or light meal.

5. Open-Faced Hummus Sandwich
Start with a piece of whole-grain bread, top with a nice layer of oil-free hummus, and finish with fresh avocado and cucumber slices.

6. Fruit and Veggie Salads
Eating salad doesn't have to be boring! Having a nice greens base prepared ahead of time and stored in the fridge is a must. Start with a bed of greens (spinach, romaine, or spring mix) and pile the fresh ingredients high. In this salad, we used a combination of green grapes, heirloom tomatoes, freshly-cut pineapple chunks, and organic apples.

7. No-Bake Cookies With Dates
Dates pack an excellent punch when it comes to energy. With more potassium than a banana, dates are a bite-sized roll of goodness that can give you the whole-food energy you need.   mixes raw almonds, walnuts, dates, vanilla extract, old-fashioned oats, and dark chocolate chips for a wonderful combination of flavor that can serve as an on-the-go snack or a sweet treat after a meal.You can also try these raw choco bites made of oats, dates, and carrots.

8. Fast Pita Pizzas

Top pita bread with tomato sauce, basil, oregano, and your favorite toppings and pop it into a 250°F toaster oven for five minutes.

9. Quick Bean Salads

Keep a big batch of bean salad in your fridge for snacking or as the base for a last-minute meal. Whether you make this quick black bean salad, our corn salad, or your own combination, these hearty bean salads are satisfying and easy to whip up.

10. Leftover Cooked Potatoes or Sweet Potatoes

These are great on their own or topped with salsa or leftover chili. Prepare extra potatoes when you're cooking, or you can quickly microwave a few if you don't have any leftovers in the fridge.

Stocking healthy snacks while keeping products with ingredients you can't pronounce out of your pantry is the key to success in the whole-food, plant-based diet. Do this and you will be ready to take on the world, one healthy day at a time!

BEST INSTANT POT COOKBOOKS & PLANT-BASED DIET

The best-selling Instant Pot makes cooking delicious meals a snap! But finding Plant-Based Diet recipes that are both inspiring and trustworthy has proven difficult, until now. The Complete Plant-Based Diet Instant Pot Cookbook 2020 presents a collection of quick and easy Plant-Based recipes that cover each meal of the day, offering tried-and-true dishes with a modern twist. And best of all, they're all well-tested and authorized by Instant Pot. With beautiful attractive package, this book is an indulgence for home cooks who live a plant-based lifestyle as well as healthy eaters looking to incorporate more meatless Mondays into their week.

BREAKFAST

Cinnamon Apple Porridge

Serves: 4

Ingredients:
- Quinoa – 1 cup, rinsed
- Water – 1 ½ cups
- Maple syrup – 2 Tbsp.
- Ground cinnamon – 2 Tbsp.
- Vanilla extract – ½ tsp.
- Salt – ¼ tsp.
- Apple – 1, chopped
- Nondairy milk – ½ to 1 cup

Directions:
1. In the Instant Pot, stir together the apple, salt, vanilla, cinnamon, maple syrup, water, and quinoa.
2. Cover the Instant Pot.
3. Cook on High for 7 minutes. (all the times are at sea level).
4. Do a natural release and open.
5. Stir in the milk and serve.

Nutritional Facts Per Serving:
- Calories: 232
- Fat: 4g
- Carb: 45g
- Protein: 7g

Peanut Butter & Chocolate Steel Cut Oats

Serves: 4

Ingredients:
- Steel cut oats – 2 cups
- Water – 2 ½ cups
- Nondairy milk – 2 ½ cups, plus more as needed
- Salt – ¼ tsp.
- Chocolate chips – ¼ cup
- Peanut butter – ¼ cup
- Maple syrup – 2 Tbsp.

Directions:
1. In the Instant Pot, combine the chocolate chips, salt, 2 cups of milk, water, and oats. Stir to mix.
2. Cover the Instant Pot.
3. Cook on High for 10 minutes.
4. Do a natural release and open
5. Add the remaining milk. Stir in maple syrup and peanut butter.
6. Serve.

Nutritional Facts Per Serving:
- Calories: 357
- Fat: 16g
- Carb: 45g
- Protein: 11g

Fruity Quinoa & Granola Bowls

Serves: 4

Ingredients:
- Quinoa – 1 cup, rinsed
- Water – 1 ½ cups
- Maple syrup – 2 Tbsp. plus more for topping
- Vanilla extract – 1 tsp.
- Ground cinnamon – ½ tsp.
- Pinch salt
- Nondairy milk – ½ to 1 cup
- Granola – 2 cups
- Fresh fruit compote – 2 cups
- Sliced bananas and toasted almonds for topping

Directions:
1. In the Instant Pot, combine cinnamon, salt, vanilla, maple syrup, water, and quinoa.
2. Cover the Instant Pot.
3. Cook on High for 7 minutes.
4. Do a natural release when done
5. Remove the lid and stir the quinoa. Add the milk.
6. Spoon the quinoa mix into the bowls and top with compote, granola, and other toppings.
7. Serve.

Nutritional Facts Per Serving:
- Calories: 507
- Fat: 7g
- Carb: 104g
- Protein: 10g

Oats With Milk And Blueberry

Serves: 4

Ingredients:
- Steel cut oats – 2 cups
- Water – 4 ½ cups
- Nondairy milk – ½ to 1 cup
- Agave or maple syrup – 2 Tbsp.
- Salt – ¼ tsp.
- Chia seeds – ¼ to ½ cup
- Chopped walnuts – 1 cup
- Fresh blueberries – 1 cup

Directions:
1. In the Instant Pot, stir together the water and oats.
2. Cover the Instant Pot.
3. Cook on High for 10 minutes.
4. Do a natural release.
5. Open and add the milk. Stir in agave and salt.
6. Top with blueberries, walnuts, and chia seeds and serve.

Nutritional Facts Per Serving:
- Calories: 328
- Fat: 13g
- Carb: 47g
- Protein: 10g

Kale And Sweet Potato Mini Quiche

Serves: 7

Ingredients:
- Firm tofu – 1 (14-ounce0 package) lightly pressed
- Nondairy milk – ¼ cup
- Nutritional yeast – ¼ cup
- Cornstarch – 1 Tbsp.
- Sea salt – ½ tsp. plus more for seasoning
- Garlic powder – ½ tsp.
- Onion powder – ½ tsp.
- Ground turmeric – ½ tsp.
- Shredded sweet potato – ½ cup
- Kale leaves – 1 handful, chopped
- Water – 1 cup, plus 1 Tbsp.
- Vegan-buttered toast for serving
- Freshly ground black pepper

Directions:
1. Use nonstick spray to coal an 8 ¼-silicone egg-bites mold. Set aside.
2. In a food processor, combine turmeric, onion powder, garlic powder, salt, cornstarch, yeast, milk, and tofu. Blend until smooth.
3. Press Sauté on the Instant Pot. Add 1 tbsp. water, kale, and sweet potato.
4. Sauté for 1 to 2 minutes.
5. Stir the veggies into the tofu mixture and spoon the mixture into the prepared mold. Cover the mold tightly with aluminum foil.
6. Place on the trivet. Add the remaining 1 cup of water to the Instant Pot and place the trivet with the mold in the Instant Pot.
7. Cover the Instant Pot. Cook on High for 15 minutes.
8. Do a natural release, then do a quick release.
9. Remove the lid and cool. Serve quiches with toasts.

Nutritional Facts Per Serving:
- Calories: 150
- Fat: 5g
- Carb: 16g
- Protein: 14g

Poblano-Sweet Potato Hash

Serves: 4

Ingredients:
- Sweet potatoes – 2, cut into large dice
- Water – 1 cup
- Extra-firm tofu – 1(14-ounce) package, pressed, then crumbled in a food processor
- Ground turmeric – 1 tsp.
- Smoked paprika – ½ tsp.
- Sea salt – ½ tsp.
- Olive oil – 1 to 2 Tbsp.
- Small onion – 1, diced
- Bell pepper – 1, diced
- Poblano peppers – 2, roasted, cut into large dice
- Garlic – 2 cloves, minced
- Montreal chicken seasoning – 1 ½ tsp.

Directions:
1. In the Instant Pot, combine the water and sweet potatoes.
2. Cover the Instant Pot.
3. Cook on High for 2 minutes.
4. Meanwhile, heat a skillet on a stovetop. Add salt, paprika, turmeric, and tofu crumbles. Stir-fry for 5 minutes. Remove from the heat and set aside.
5. Do a quick release. Drain and set aside.
6. Press Sauté on the Instant Pot.
7. Add 1 tbsp. oil, bell pepper, and onion. Stir-fry for 2 to 3 minutes.
8. Add the seasoning, garlic, and poblanos. Cook for 1 minute more.
9. Add 1 tbsp. oil if necessary. Add the sweet potato back to the pot and cook for 2 to 3 minutes.
10. Turn off the Instant Pot and stir in the tofu. Mix and serve.

Nutritional Facts Per Serving:
- Calories: 238
- Fat: 13g
- Carb: 22g
- Protein: 12g

Tempeh Sausage

Serves: 4

Ingredients:
- Olive oil – 1 Tbsp.
- Unflavored tempeh – 1 (8-ounce) package
- Vegan Worcestershire sauce – 2 tsp.
- Smoked paprika – 1 ½ tsp.
- Onion powder – 1 tsp.
- Garlic powder - 1 tsp.
- Dried sage – 1 tsp.
- Dried oregano – ½ tsp.
- Salt – ½ tsp. plus more as needed
- Freshly ground black pepper – ¼ tsp.
- Pinch of chili powder
- Water -1 cup

Directions:
1. Press Sauté on the Instant Pot. Add oil.
2. Crumble the tempeh and add to the hot oil. Stir to coat.
3. Add the chili powder, salt, pepper, oregano, sage, garlic powder, onion powder, paprika, and Worcestershire sauce.
4. Press Cancel and add the water. Deglaze the pot.
5. Cook on High for 3 minutes.
6. Do a quick release.
7. Remove the lid and cook on Sauté to remove the remaining liquid.
8. Serve.

Nutritional Facts Per Serving:
- Calories: 161
- Fat: 10g
- Carb: 8g
- Protein: 12g

Cinnamon Apple Porridge

Serves: 4

Ingredients:
- 1 cup quinoa, rinsed
- 1½ cups water
- 2 tablespoons maple syrup
- 2 tablespoons ground cinnamon
- ½ teaspoon vanilla extract
- ¼ to ½ teaspoon salt
- 1 apple, chopped
- ½ to 1 cup nondairy milk

Directions:
1. In your Instant Pot®, stir together the quinoa, water, maple syrup, cinnamon, vanilla, salt, and apple (if you want it soft). Lock the lid and turn the steam release handle to Sealing. Using the Manual function, set the cooker to High Pressure for 8 minutes (7 minutes at sea level).
2. When the cook time is complete, let the pressure release naturally for 10 minutes; quick release any remaining pressure.
3. Carefully remove the lid and stir in as much milk as needed to make it creamy.
4. If you didn't cook the apples, add them now and put the cover back on for 1 to 2 minutes to warm them.

Nutritional Facts Per Serving:
- Calories: 232;
- Total fat: 4g;
- Saturated fat: 0g;
- Sodium: 196mg;
- Carbs: 45g;
- Fiber: 6g;
- Protein: 7g

Peanut Butter & Chocolate Steel Cut Oats

Serves: 4 TO 6

Ingredients:
- 2 cups steel cut oats
- 2½ cups water
- 2½ cups nondairy milk, divided, plus more as needed
- ¼ teaspoon salt
- ¼ cup chocolate chips
- ¼ cup peanut butter
- 2 tablespoons agave, or maple syrup

Directions:
1. 1. In the Instant Pot®, combine the oats, water, 2 cups of milk, the salt, and chocolate chips. Stir to mix. Lock the lid and turn the steam release handle to Sealing. Using the Manual function, set the cooker to High Pressure for 12 minutes (10 minutes at sea level).
2. 2. When the cook time is complete, turn off the pressure cooker. Let the pressure release naturally for 10 minutes; quick release any remaining pressure.
3. 3. Add the remaining ½ cup of milk (more if you want the oats thinner). Stir in the peanut butter and agave (I like my peanut butter in thick swirls!) and enjoy.
4. TECHNIQUE TIP: Make sure the inner pot of your pressure cooker is never filled more than halfway when cooking oats or the foam may clog the pressure release valve.

Nutritional Facts Per Serving:
- Calories: 357;
- Total fat: 16g;
- Saturated fat: 5g;
- Sodium: 346mg;
- Carbs: 45g;
- Fiber: 6g;
- Protein: 11g

Fruity Quinoa & Granola Bowls

Serves: 4

Ingredients:
- 1 cup quinoa, rinsed
- 1½ cups water
- 2 tablespoons maple syrup, plus more for topping (optional)
- 1 teaspoon vanilla extract
- ½ teaspoon ground cinnamon
- Pinch salt
- ½ to 1 cup nondairy milk
- 2 cups granola (any variety)
- 2 cups Fresh Fruit Compote
- Sliced bananas, for topping (optional)
- Toasted walnuts, for topping (optional)

Directions:
1. 1. In your Instant Pot®, combine the quinoa, water, maple syrup, vanilla, cinnamon, and salt. Lock the lid and turn the steam release handle to Sealing. Using the Manual function, set the cooker to High Pressure for 8 minutes (7 minutes at sea level).
2. 2. When the cook time is complete, let the pressure release naturally for 10 minutes; quick release any remaining pressure.
3. 3. Carefully remove the lid and stir the quinoa. Add enough milk to get the desired consistency. Spoon the quinoa mix into bowls and top with granola, compote, and any additional toppings, as desired.
4. MAKE-AHEAD TIP: The quinoa and compote can be made during your weekly meal prep and stored separately. Simply reheat and assemble for a delicious breakfast!

Nutritional Facts Per Serving:
- Calories: 507;
- Total fat: 7g;
- Saturated fat: 2g;
- Sodium: 100mg;
- Carbs: 104g;
- Fiber: 9g;
- Protein: 10g

Healthy-Yet-Tasty Oats

Serves: 4 TO 6

Ingredients:
- 2 cups steel cut oats
- 4½ cups water
- ½ to 1 cup nondairy milk
- 2 tablespoons agave, or maple syrup (optional)
- ¼ teaspoon salt (optional)
- ¼ to ½ cup chia seeds
- 1 cup chopped walnuts
- 1 cup fresh blueberries

Directions:
1. In your Instant Pot®, stir together the oats and water. Lock the lid and turn the steam release handle to Sealing. Using the Manual function, set the cooker to High Pressure for 12 minutes (10 minutes at sea level).
2. When the cook time is complete, turn off the Instant Pot®. Let the pressure release naturally for 10 minutes; quick release any remaining pressure.
3. Carefully remove the lid and add the milk. Stir in the agave and salt (if using) and top with the chia seeds, walnuts, and blueberries.

Nutritional Facts Per Serving:
- Calories: 328;
- Total fat: 13g;
- Saturated fat: 1g;
- Sodium: 198mg;
- Carbs: 47g;
- Fiber: 11g;
- Protein: 10g

Kale & Sweet Potato Mini Quiche

Serves: makes 7 quiches

Ingredients:
- 1 (14-ounce) package firm tofu, lightly pressed
- ¼ cup nondairy milk
- ¼ cup nutritional yeast
- 1 tablespoon cornstarch
- ½ to 1 teaspoon kala namak, or sea salt, plus more for seasoning
- ½ teaspoon garlic powder
- ½ teaspoon onion powder
- ½ teaspoon ground turmeric
- ½ cup shredded sweet potato
- Handful kale leaves, chopped small
- 1 cup plus 1 tablespoon water
- Vegan-buttered toast, for serving
- Freshly ground black pepper

Directions:
1. Lightly coat an 8¼-inch silicone egg-bites mold with nonstick spray and set aside. In a food processor, combine the tofu, milk, yeast, cornstarch, kala namak, garlic powder, onion powder, and turmeric. Blend until smooth.
2. On your Instant Pot®, select Sauté Low. When the display reads "Hot," add the sweet potato, kale, and 1 tablespoon of water. Sauté for 1 to 2 minutes (you may need to turn off the Instant Pot® if the vegetables start to stick to the bottom, but that's okay because it stays hot). Stir the veggies into the tofu mixture and spoon the mixture into the prepared mold. Cover the mold tightly with aluminum foil and place on a trivet. Add the remaining 1 cup of water to the inner pot and use the trivet's handles to lower the trivet and mold into the pot.
3. Lock the lid and turn the steam release handle to Sealing. Using the Manual function, set the cooker to High Pressure for 18 minutes (15 minutes at sea level). When the cook time is complete, let the pressure release naturally for 10 minutes; quick release any remaining pressure.
4. Carefully remove the lid. Remove the silicone mold from the Instant Pot® and pull off the foil. Leave the mold on the trivet and let cool for a few minutes. The bites will continue to firm as they cool. When ready to eat, schmear the tofu bites onto a piece of vegan-buttered toast and top with a little salt and pepper.
5. SUBSTITUTION TIP: Use your favorite veggies here! Spinach and tomato is my second favorite combination (squeeze the excess liquid from the tomatoes with a paper towel or the tofu won't firm up all the way).

Nutritional Facts Per Serving:
- Calories: 150;
- Total fat: 5g;
- Saturated fat: 1g;
- Sodium: 46mg;
- Carbs: 16g;
- Fiber: 5g;
- Protein: 14g

GRAINS, BEANS, AND LEGUMES

Green Chile Baked Beans

Serves: 4 TO 6

Ingredients:
- ¼ cup blackstrap molasses
- ¼ cup maple syrup
- ¼ cup packed light brown sugar
- 2 tablespoons ketchup
- 1 tablespoon vegan Worcestershire sauce
- 1 tablespoon olive oil
- 1 small sweet onion, cut into large dice
- 3 or 4 garlic cloves, minced
- 1 teaspoon salt
- 1 pound dried navy beans, soaked in water overnight, rinsed, and drained
- 1½ cups diced roasted green chiles (freshly roasted Hatch or poblanos, or from a can)
- 1 teaspoon apple cider vinegar

Directions:
1. In a small bowl, whisk the molasses, maple syrup, brown sugar, ketchup, and Worcestershire sauce. Set aside.
2. On your Instant Pot®, select Sauté Low. When the display reads "Hot," add the oil and heat until it shimmers. Add the onion and garlic. Turn off the Instant Pot® and sauté the veggies for 1 to 2 minutes, stirring frequently. Add the salt, beans, and molasses mix, stirring well. Lock the lid and turn the steam release handle to Sealing. Using the Manual function, set the cooker to High Pressure for 35 minutes (30 minutes at sea level).
3. When the cook time is complete, let the pressure release naturally for 20 minutes, or until the pin drops.
4. Carefully remove the lid and stir. Select Sauté Medium. Stir in the green chiles and simmer the beans for 5 to 10 minutes, or until the sauce thickens.
5. Stir in the vinegar and serve.

Nutritional Facts Per Serving:
- Calories: 435;
- Total fat: 4g;
- Saturated fat: 1g;
- Sodium: 947mg;
- Carbs: 89g;
- Fiber:19g;
- Protein: 21g

Mexican Black Beans

Serves: 6 TO 8

Ingredients:
- 1 to 2 tablespoons olive oil
- 1 small onion, diced
- 3 or 4 garlic cloves, diced
- 1 tablespoon ground cumin
- 1 teaspoon dried oregano
- 1 teaspoon chili powder
- 1 cup diced roasted green chiles (freshly roasted Hatch chiles or from a can)
- 3 cups DIY Vegetable Stock, or store-bought stock
- 2 cups dried black beans, rinsed but not soaked
- ½ to 1 teaspoon salt, plus more as needed
- 2 tablespoons freshly squeezed lime juice
- ¼ cup fresh cilantro leaves, chopped

Directions:
1. On your Instant Pot®, select Sauté Low. When the display reads "Hot," add the oil and onion. Sauté for 1 to 2 minutes, turning off the Instant Pot® after about 1 minute. Add the garlic. Sauté for 30 seconds. Stir in the cumin, oregano, and chili powder, and cook for another 30 seconds or so until the spices "bloom" (become very fragrant). Add the green chiles, stock, and black beans, stirring well. Lock the lid and turn the steam release handle to Sealing. Using the Manual function, set the cooker to High Pressure for 35 minutes (30 minutes at sea level).
2. When the cook time is complete, let the pressure release naturally for 20 minutes, or until the pin drops.
3. Carefully remove the lid and stir. Add the salt, lime juice, and cilantro. Stir again and serve.

Nutritional Facts Per Serving:
- Calories: 287;
- Total fat: 5g;
- Saturated fat: 2g;
- Sodium: 439mg;
- Carbs: 50g;
- Fiber: 11g;
- Protein: 17g

Refried Pinto Beans

Serves: 6 TO 8

Ingredients:
- 1 tablespoon olive oil
- 1 onion, quartered
- 3 garlic cloves, peeled
- 1 pound dried pinto beans, rinsed
- 2 quarts DIY Vegetable Stock, or store-bought stock
- 1 teaspoon ground cumin
- 1 teaspoon dried Mexican oregano
- ½ teaspoon chili powder
- ¼ teaspoon freshly ground black pepper
- 1 tablespoon freshly squeezed lime juice
- 1 tablespoon salt, plus more as needed

Directions:
1. In your Instant Pot®, combine the oil, onion, garlic, beans, stock, cumin, oregano, chili powder, and pepper. Lock the lid and turn the steam release handle to Sealing. Using the Manual function, set the cooker to High Pressure for 38 minutes (32 minutes at sea level).
2. When the cook time is complete, let the pressure release naturally for about 20 minutes, or until the pin drops.
3. Carefully remove the lid and use a ladle to remove most of the remaining liquid, saving it. Using an immersion blender, blend the beans until smooth, adding the cooking water back in as needed.
4. Stir in the lime juice and salt.

Nutritional Facts Per Serving:
- Calories: 310;
- Total fat: 6g;
- Saturated fat: 3g;
- Sodium: 720mg;
- Carbs: 53g;
- Fiber: 12g;
- Protein: 17g

Red Beans & Rice

Serves: 4 TO 6

Ingredients:
- 1 tablespoon olive oil
- 1 red onion, diced
- 1 bell pepper, any color, diced
- 2 celery stalks, sliced
- 4 or 5 garlic cloves, minced
- 2 bay leaves
- 2 teaspoons Cajun seasoning
- ½ teaspoon dried oregano
- ½ teaspoon dried parsley
- 2 cups dried red beans
- 4 cups DIY Vegetable Stock, or store-bought stock
- Salt
- Freshly ground black pepper
- 4 to 5 cups cooked white rice
- Chopped fresh parsley, for garnishing
- Hot sauce, for serving

Directions:
1. On your Instant Pot®, select Sauté Low. When the display reads "Hot," add the oil and heat until it shimmers. Add the red onion, bell pepper, and celery. Cook for 3 to 4 minutes, stirring frequently. Turn off the Instant Pot® and add the garlic, bay leaves, Cajun seasoning, oregano, and dried parsley. Continue to cook for 1 minute more, stirring.
2. Stir in the beans and stock. Lock the lid and turn the steam release handle to Sealing. Using the Manual function, set the cooker to High Pressure for 40 minutes (34 minutes at sea level).
3. When the cook time is complete, let the pressure release naturally for about 25 minutes, or until the pin drops.
4. Carefully remove the lid, and remove and discard the bay leaves. Taste and season with salt and pepper, as needed. Serve with rice and top with parsley and hot sauce.

Nutritional Facts Per Serving:
- Calories: 609;
- Total fat: 5g;
- Saturated fat: 1g;
- Sodium: 312mg;
- Carbs: 116g;
- Fiber: 15g;
- Protein: 26g

Chickpea Basil Salad

Serves: 2 TO 4

Ingredients:
- 1 cup dried chickpeas, rinsed
- 1 quart water, or enough to cover the chickpeas by 3 to 4 inches
- 1 cup fresh basil leaves, chopped or sliced
- 1½ cups grape tomatoes, halved
- 2 to 3 tablespoons balsamic vinegar
- ½ teaspoon garlic powder
- ½ teaspoon salt, plus more as needed

Directions:
1. In your Instant Pot®, combine the chickpeas and water. Lock the lid and turn the steam release handle to Sealing. Using the Manual function, set the cooker to High Pressure for 45 minutes (38 minutes at sea level).
2. When the cook time is complete, let the pressure release naturally for 20 minutes; quick release any remaining pressure.
3. Carefully remove the lid and drain the chickpeas. Refrigerate to cool (unless you want to serve this warm, which is good, too).
4. While the chickpeas cool, in a large bowl, stir together the basil, tomatoes, vinegar, garlic powder, and salt. Add the beans, stir to combine, and serve.

Nutritional Facts Per Serving:
- Calories: 396;
- Total fat: 6g;
- Saturated fat: 1g;
- Sodium: 613mg;
- Carbs: 67g;
- Fiber: 19g;
- Protein: 21g

Green Chile Chickpeas

Serves: 4 TO 6

Ingredients:
- 2 cups dried chickpeas, rinsed
- 6 cups water
- 1 small tomato, diced
- 1 cup diced roasted green chiles (freshly roasted or from a can)
- 2 teaspoons freshly squeezed lemon juice
- 1 teaspoon ground cumin
- ½ teaspoon chili powder, plus more as needed
- ½ to 1 teaspoon salt
- ½ teaspoon garlic powder
- ½ teaspoon red pepper flakes
- ½ teaspoon smoked paprika
- ½ teaspoon onion powder
- ¼ teaspoon dried oregano
- ¼ teaspoon freshly ground black pepper

Directions:
1. In your Instant Pot®, combine the chickpeas and water. Lock the lid and turn the steam release handle to Sealing. Using the Manual function, set the cooker to High Pressure for 45 minutes (38 minutes at sea level).
2. When the cook time is complete, let the pressure release naturally for 20 minutes; quick release any remaining pressure.
3. Carefully remove the lid and drain the chickpeas, reserving 1 to 2 tablespoons of the cooking water. Return the chickpeas to the Instant Pot® (be careful, the inner pot will be hot). Stir in the tomato, green chiles, lemon juice, cumin, chili powder, salt, garlic powder, red pepper flakes, paprika, onion powder, oregano, and black pepper. If they're too dry, add the reserved cooking water.
4. On your Instant Pot®, select Sauté Low and cook for 3 to 4 minutes. You may need to turn the Instant Pot® off if anything starts to burn at the bottom. Put the lid back on and turn on the Keep Warm function. Let the chickpeas sit in all that goodness for 5 minutes—then they're ready.

Nutritional Facts Per Serving:
- Calories: 416;
- Total fat: 6g;
- Saturated fat: 1g;
- Sodium: 754mg;
- Carbs: 71g;
- Fiber: 18g;
- Protein: 24g

Mediterranean Lentils

Serves: 2 TO 4

Ingredients:
- 1 tablespoon olive oil
- 1 small sweet or yellow onion, diced
- 1 garlic clove, diced
- 1 teaspoon dried oregano
- ½ teaspoon ground cumin
- ½ teaspoon dried parsley
- ½ teaspoon salt, plus more as needed
- ¼ teaspoon freshly ground black pepper, plus more as needed
- 1 tomato, diced
- 1 cup brown or green lentils
- 2½ cups DIY Vegetable Stock, or store-bought stock
- 1 bay leaf

Directions:
1. On your Instant Pot®, select Sauté Low. When the display reads "Hot," add the oil and heat until it shimmers. Add the onion. Cook for 3 to 4 minutes until soft. Turn off the Instant Pot® and add the garlic, oregano, cumin, parsley, salt, and pepper. Cook until fragrant, about 1 minute.
2. Stir in the tomato, lentils, stock, and bay leaf. Lock the lid and turn the steam release handle to Sealing. Using the Manual function, set the cooker to High Pressure for 18 minutes (15 minutes at sea level).
3. When the cook time is complete, let the pressure release naturally for 10 minutes; quick release any remaining pressure.
4. Carefully remove the lid, and remove and discard the bay leaf. Taste and season with more salt and pepper, as needed. If there's too much liquid remaining, select Sauté Medium or High and cook until it evaporates.

Nutritional Facts Per Serving:
- Calories: 426;
- Total fat: 8g;
- Saturated fat: 1g;
- Sodium: 592mg;
- Carbs: 64g;
- Fiber: 31g;
- Protein: 26g

Smoky Butternut Lentils

Serves: 4 TO 6

Ingredients:
- 1 tablespoon olive oil
- ½ onion, diced
- 1 garlic clove, minced
- 1 small butternut squash, peeled and cubed (about 3 cups)
- 1¾ cups water, or DIY Vegetable Stock, or store-bought stock
- 1 cup red lentils, rinsed
- 1 teaspoon smoked paprika
- ½ to 1 teaspoon salt
- ½ teaspoon ground cumin
- Pinch chili powder

Directions:
1. On your Instant Pot®, select Sauté Low. When the display reads "Hot," add the oil and heat until it shimmers. Add the onion. Cook for 2 to 3 minutes, stirring frequently. Turn off the Instant Pot® and add the garlic. Cook for 30 seconds, stirring.
2. Stir in the squash, water, lentils, paprika, salt, cumin, and chili powder. Lock the lid and turn the steam release handle to Sealing. Using the Manual function, set the cooker to High Pressure for 10 minutes (9 minutes at sea level).
3. When the cook time is complete, let the pressure release naturally for 10 minutes; quick release any remaining pressure.
4. Carefully remove the lid and stir. The lentils and butternut will break down quickly—no need to mash. Just stir and, when they're smooth, taste and adjust the seasonings, as needed.

Nutritional Facts Per Serving:
- Calories: 256;
- Total fat: 4g;
- Saturated fat: 1g;
- Sodium: 591mg;
- Carbs: 43g;
- Fiber: 17g;
- Protein: 14g

Spicy Southwestern Lentils

Serves: 4 TO 6

Ingredients:
- 1 tablespoon olive oil
- 1 small onion, diced
- 1 or 2 garlic cloves, finely diced
- 1 bell pepper, any color, diced
- 2 Roma tomatoes, diced
- 2 cups DIY Vegetable Stock, or store-bought stock
- 1 cup green or brown lentils, rinsed and drained
- ½ to 1 teaspoon salt, plus more as needed
- 1 teaspoon ground cumin
- 1 teaspoon chili powder
- 1 teaspoon smoked paprika
- 1 cup well chopped kale
- Freshly ground black pepper

Directions:
1. On your Instant Pot®, select Sauté Low. When the display reads "Hot," add the oil and heat until it shimmers. Add the onion. Sauté for 1 to 2 minutes and then turn off the Instant Pot®. Add the garlic. Cook for about 30 seconds, stirring (don't let it burn).
2. Add the bell pepper, tomatoes, stock, lentils, salt, cumin, chili powder, and paprika. Lock the lid and turn the steam release handle to Sealing. Using the Manual function, set the cooker to High Pressure for 15 minutes (13 minutes at sea level).
3. When the cook time is complete, let the Instant Pot® go into Keep Warm mode and let the pressure release naturally for 10 minutes; quick release any remaining pressure.
4. Carefully remove the lid and stir in the kale, which will wilt after 1 to 2 minutes. Taste and season with salt and pepper, as needed.

Nutritional Facts Per Serving:
- Calories: 247;
- Total fat: 5g;
- Saturated fat: 1g;
- Sodium: 604mg;
- Carbs: 39g;
- Fiber: 17g;
- Protein: 14g

Cilantro Lime Brown Rice

Serves: 4 TO 6

Ingredients:
- 2 cups brown rice, rinsed and drained
- 2½ cups water
- ⅓ cup fresh cilantro, chopped, plus more as needed
- Juice of 1 lime
- Zest of 1 lime
- Dash ground cumin
- Salt

Directions:
1. In your Instant Pot®, combine the rice and water. Lock the lid and turn the steam release handle to Sealing. Using the Manual function, set the cooker to High Pressure for 22 minutes (19 minutes at sea level).
2. When the cook time is complete, let the pressure release naturally for 10 minutes while the Instant Pot® goes into Keep Warm mode; quick release any remaining pressure.
3. Carefully remove the lid and stir in the cilantro, lime juice and zest, and cumin. Season to taste with salt.

Nutritional Facts Per Serving:
- Calories: 344;
- Total fat: 3g;
- Saturated fat: 1g;
- Sodium: 67mg;
- Carbs: 72g;
- Fiber: 3g;
- Protein: 7g

Biryani Rice

Serves: 3

Ingredients:
- Red onion – ¼ cup, diced
- Garlic clove – 1, minced
- Turmeric powder – ½ tsp.
- Cumin seeds – 1 tsp.
- Cinnamon stick – 1
- Salt – ¼ tsp.
- Brown rice – 1 cup, soaked 10 minutes, then drained
- Water – 1 ½ cups
- Raisins – ¼ cup
- Mint – ¼ cup, chopped
- Raw cashew, chopped
- Fresh mint leaves
- Fresh cilantro

Directions:
1. Press Sauté on your Instant Pot.
2. Add cumin seeds, diced red onion, minced garlic, turmeric powder, cinnamon, and salt to the Instant Pot.
3. Stir-fry for 1 minute.
4. Add brown rice and stir.
5. Cover the Instant Pot.
6. Cook on Multigrain for 25 minutes.
7. Do a quick release and open.
8. Add raisins and chopped mint. Mix.
9. Serve the rice garnished with fresh mint leaves and chopped cashews.

Nutritional Facts Per Serving:
- Calories: 420
- Fat: 3g
- Carb: 92.1g
- Protein: 8.3g

Spanish Rice

Serves: 4

Ingredients:
- White rice – 2 cups
- Vegetable oil – 1 Tbsp.
- Green onions – 6
- Diced tomatoes – 1 can
- Red onion – 1
- Cilantro – 1 tsp.
- Lemon zest – 1 tsp.
- Water – 3 cups

Directions:
1. Add tomatoes to the Instant Pot.
2. Add chopped onion and rest of the .
3. Cover the Instant Pot.
4. Cook for 5 minutes on High.
5. Open and check. If the rice isn't done, then cook for 2 minutes more.
6. Do a natural release.
7. Stir the rice and serve.

Nutritional Facts Per Serving:
- Calories: 394
- Fat: 4.2g
- Carb: 80g
- Protein: 7.7g

Potato And Green Bean Salad

Serves: 6

Ingredients:
- Large potatoes – 3, skinned and chopped
- Frozen green beans – 2 large
- Mushrooms – 1 cup
- Water – 1 ½ cup
- Olive oil – 2 Tbsp.
- Dash of sea salt
- Splash of lemon juice
- Pepper to taste

Directions:
1. Add lemon juice, water, salt, pepper, mushrooms, and potatoes to the Instant Pot. Place a steamer basket.
2. Place green beans on top of the steamer basket and drizzle with oil.
3. Cover and cook on High for 5 to 7 minutes.
4. Open and pour the beans into a strainer, then place on a large bowl.
5. Mix the green beans and the rest of thefrom the Instant Pot. Mix.
6. Serve.

Nutritional Facts Per Serving:
- Calories: 218
- Fat: 5.1g
- Carb: 40.4g
- Protein: 6.3g

Three Bean Delight

Serves: 4

Ingredients:
- Chickpeas – 1 can
- Black beans – 1 can
- Green beans – 2 cups
- Garlic powder – 1 Tbsp.
- Celery – 2 stalks
- Small red onion – 1
- Coconut oil – 4 Tbsp.
- Sugar – 2 Tbsp.
- Apple cider vinegar – 5 Tbsp.
- Salt and pepper

Directions:
1. Open and drain both cans of beans and slice the celery. Chop onion.
2. Add theseto the Instant Pot. Place a steamer and add the green beans on top.
3. Cover the Instant Pot
4. Cook on High for 10 minutes.
5. Do a natural release.
6. Open and add the green beans with the rest of the salad.
7. Serve.

Nutritional Facts Per Serving:
- Calories: 676
- Fat: 19g
- Carb: 100g
- Protein: 30.6g

Green Chili Baked Beans

Serves: 4

Ingredients:
- Blackstrap molasses – ¼ cup
- Maple syrup – ¼ cup
- Packed light brown sugar – ¼ cup
- Ketchup – 2 Tbsp.
- Vegan Worcestershire sauce – 1 Tbsp.
- Olive oil – 1 tbsp.
- Sweet onion – 1 small, chopped
- Garlic – 3 to 4, minced
- Salt – 1 tsp.
- Dried navy beans – 1 pound, soaked in water overnight, rinsed and drained
- Diced roasted green chilies – 1 ½ cups
- Apple cider vinegar – 1 tsp.

Directions:
1. In a bowl, whisk the sauce, ketchup, brown sugar, maple syrup, and molasses.
2. Press Sauté on the Instant Pot and add oil.
3. Add onion and garlic.
4. Stir-fry for 2 minutes.
5. Add molasses mix, beans, and salt and mix.
6. Cover the Instant Pot.
7. Cook on High for 30 minutes.
8. Do a natural release.
9. Open the lid and press Sauté.
10. Stir in green chilies and simmer until thickens about 5 to 10 minutes.

Nutritional Facts Per Serving:
- Calories: 435
- Fat: 4g
- Carb: 89g
- Protein: 21g

Mexican Black Beans

Serves: 3

Ingredients:
- Olive oil - 2 Tbsp.
- Small onion – 1, diced
- Garlic – 3 to 4 cloves, diced
- Ground cumin – 1 Tbsp.
- Dried oregano – 1 tsp.
- Chili powder – 1 tsp.
- Diced roasted green chiles – 1 cup
- Vegetable stock - 3 cups
- Dried black beans – 2 cups, rinsed but not soaked
- Salt – 1 tsp. plus more to taste
- Lime juice – 2 Tbsp.
- Fresh cilantro leaves – ¼ cup, chopped

Directions:
1. Press Sauté on the Instant Pot. Add oil.
2. Add onion and stir-fry for 2 minutes.
3. Add garlic and stir-fry for 30 seconds.
4. Stir in chili powder, oregano, and cumin — Cook for 30 seconds.
5. Add the black beans, stock, green chiles, and mix.
6. Cover the Instant Pot.
7. Cook on High for 30 minutes.
8. Do a natural release.
9. Open and add cilantro, lime juice, and salt.
10. Serve.

Nutritional Facts Per Serving:
- Calories: 287
- Fat: 5g
- Carb: 50g
- Protein: 17g

Refried Pinto Beans

Serves: 6

Ingredients:
- Olive oil - 1 Tbsp.
- Onion – 1, quartered
- Garlic – 3 cloves, peeled
- Dried pinto beans – 1 pound, rinsed
- Vegetable stock – 2 quarts
- Ground cumin – 1 tsp.
- Dried Mexican oregano – 1 tsp.
- Chili powder – ½ tsp.
- Ground black pepper – ¼ tsp.
- Lime juice – 1 Tbsp.
- Salt – 1 Tbsp. plus more to taste

Directions:
1. In the Instant Pot, combine pepper, chili powder, oregano, cumin, stock, beans, garlic, onion, and oil.
2. Cover and cook on High for 32 minutes.
3. Do a natural release and open.
4. Remove most of the remaining liquid with a ladle.
5. Blend with a hand mixer until smooth. Add cooking water as needed.
6. Stir in salt and lime juice.
7. Serve.

Nutritional Facts Per Serving:
- Calories: 310
- Fat: 6g
- Carb: 53g
- Protein: 17g

Red Beans And Rice

Serves: 4

Ingredients:
- Olive oil – 1 Tbsp.
- Red onion – 1, diced
- Bell pepper – 1, diced
- Celery stalks – 2, sliced
- Garlic cloves – 4, minced
- Bay leaves – 2
- Cajun seasoning – 2 tsp.
- Dried oregano – ½ tsp.
- Dried parsley – ½ tsp.
- Dried red beans – 2 cups
- Vegetable stock – 4 cups
- Salt and ground black pepper
- Cooked white rice – 4 cups
- Chopped parsley and hot sauce for garnishing

Directions:
1. Press Sauté on the Instant Pot. Add oil.
2. Add celery, bell pepper, and red onion. Stir-fry for 4 minutes.
3. Add dried parsley, oregano, seasoning, bay leaves, and garlic. Cook for 1 minute.
4. Stir in beans and stock. Cover and cook on High for 34 minutes.
5. Do a natural release and open.
6. Discard the bay leaves.
7. Garnish and serve with rice.

Nutritional Facts Per Serving:
- Calories: 609
- Fat: 5g
- Carb: 116g
- Protein: 26g

Chickpea Basil Salad

Serves: 2

Ingredients:
- Dried chickpeas – 1 cup, rinsed
- Enough water to cover chickpeas by 3 to 4 inches
- Fresh basil leaves – 1 cup, chopped
- Grape tomatoes – 1 ½ cups, halved
- Balsamic vinegar – 2 Tbsp.
- Garlic powder – ½ tsp.
- Salt – ½ tsp. plus more as needed

Directions:
1. Combine the water and chickpeas in the Instant Pot.
2. Cover and cook on High for 38 minutes.
3. Do a natural release and open.
4. Drain the chickpeas. Cool.
5. Stir together the salt, garlic powder, vinegar, tomatoes, and basil in a bowl.
6. Add the beans and mix.
7. Serve.

Nutritional Facts Per Serving:
- Calories: 396
- Fat: 6g
- Carb: 67g
- Protein: 21g

Green Chili Chickpeas

Serves: 4

Ingredients:
- Dried chickpeas – 2 cups, rinsed
- Water – 6 cups
- Small tomato – 1, diced
- Diced roasted green chiles – 1 cup
- Lemon juice – 2 tsp.
- Ground cumin – 1 tsp.
- Chili powder – ½ tsp. plus more as needed
- Salt – to taste
- Garlic powder – ½ tsp.
- Red pepper flakes – ½ tsp.
- Smoked paprika – ½ tsp.
- Onion powder – ½ tsp.
- Dried oregano – ¼ tsp.
- Ground black pepper – ¼ tsp.

Directions:
1. In the Instant Pot, combine water and chickpeas.
2. Cover and cook on High for 38 minutes.
3. Do a natural release.
4. Remove the lid and drain the chickpeas. Reserve 2 tbsp. of the cooking water.
5. Return the chickpeas to the Instant Pot.
6. Stir in the black pepper, oregano, onion powder, paprika, red pepper flakes, garlic powder, salt, chili powder, cumin, lemon juice, green chilies, and tomato. Add the reserved cooking water if the mixture is too dry.
7. Press Sauté on the Instant Pot and sauté for 4 minutes.
8. Press Cancel and cover. Let the chickpeas sit for 5 minutes.
9. Serve.

Nutritional Facts Per Serving:
- Calories: 416
- Fat: 6g
- Carb: 71g
- Protein: 24g

Taco/Burrito Filling

Serves: 4 to 6

Ingredients:
- 2 cups water or unsalted vegetable broth
- 1 cup dried black beans
- 2 to 3 tablespoons chili powder
- 1 tablespoon olive oil (optional)
- 2 teaspoons onion powder
- 1 teaspoon garlic powder
- 1 teaspoon smoked paprika or 1 more teaspoon chili powder
- 1 teaspoon ground cumin (optional)
- ¼ to ½ teaspoon salt

Directions:
1. In your electric pressure cooker's cooking pot, combine the water, black beans, chili powder, olive oil (if using), onion powder, garlic powder, paprika, and cumin (if using). Close and lock the lid and ensure the pressure valve is sealed, then select High Pressure and set the time for 30 minutes.
2. Once the cook time is complete, release the pressure naturally for about 25 minutes.
3. Once all the pressure has released, carefully unlock and remove the lid. Add the salt. If the beans are not quite soft enough, or if you have too much liquid, select Sauté or Simmer and cook them, uncovered, for 15 to 20 minutes more.
4. Preparation tip: The oil is optional but highly recommended because it helps carry the spices and minimizes foaming of the beans.

Nutritional Facts Per Serving:
- Calories: 217;
- Total fat: 5g;
- Protein: 12g;
- Sodium: 186mg;
- Fiber: 13g

Curried Lentils

Serves: 4

Ingredients:
- 1 tablespoon coconut oil
- 2 tablespoons mild curry powder
- 1 teaspoon ground ginger
- ½ teaspoon ground turmeric (optional)
- 1 cup dried green lentils or brown lentils
- 3 cups water
- 1 teaspoon freshly squeezed lime juice (optional)
- ½ teaspoon salt
- Freshly ground black pepper (optional)

Directions:
1. On your electric pressure cooker, select Sauté. Add the coconut oil, curry powder, ginger, and turmeric (if using) and toss to toast for 1 minute. Add the lentils and toss with the spices. Add the water. Cancel Sauté.
2. Close and lock the lid and ensure the pressure valve is sealed, then select High Pressure and set the time for 20 minutes.
3. Once the cook time is complete, let the pressure release naturally, about 30 minutes.
4. Once all the pressure has released, carefully unlock and remove the lid. Stir in the lime juice (if using). Season with the salt and pepper, if you like.

Nutritional Facts Per Serving:
- Calories: 212;
- Total fat: 5g;
- Protein: 13g;
- Sodium: 2mg;
- Fiber: 16g

Coconut Curry Tofu

Serves: 4

Ingredients:
- 1 (13.5-ounce) can coconut milk
- ¼ cup red or green curry paste
- ¼ teaspoon salt, plus more as needed
- ¼ cup water
- 1 (14-ounce) package firm or extra-firm tofu, pressed and cubed
- 2 teaspoons unrefined sugar or brown sugar
- 2 cups chopped fresh spinach

Directions:
1. In your electric pressure cooker's cooking pot, combine the coconut milk, curry paste, salt, and water, stirring to combine. Add the tofu. Close and lock the lid and ensure the pressure valve is sealed, then select High Pressure and set the time for 3 minutes.
2. Once the cook time is complete, quick release the pressure, being careful not to get your fingers or face near the steam release.
3. Once all the pressure has released, carefully unlock and remove the lid. Stir in the sugar and spinach. Taste and season with more salt, if needed.
4. Preparation tip: Add whatever vegetables you like—cook some carrots, red bell pepper, or onion with the tofu, or stir in a handful of frozen corn or peas with the spinach and cook until they are heated through.

Nutritional Facts Per Serving:
- Calories: 438;
- Total fat: 36g;
- Protein: 13g;
- Sodium: 169mg;
- Fiber: 4g

Chipotle Chickpeas

Serves: 4 to 6

Ingredients:
- 1 cup dried chickpeas, soaked in water overnight or quick soaked for 8 minutes on High Pressure
- 2 cups water
- ¼ cup sun-dried tomatoes, chopped
- 1 to 2 tablespoons olive oil
- 2 teaspoons ground chipotle pepper
- 1½ teaspoons ground cumin
- 1½ teaspoons onion powder
- 1 teaspoon dried oregano
- ¾ teaspoon garlic powder
- ½ teaspoon smoked paprika
- ¼ to ½ teaspoon salt

Directions:
1. Drain and rinse the chickpeas, drain again, and put them in your electric pressure cooker's cooking pot.
2. Add the water, sun-dried tomatoes, olive oil, chipotle pepper, cumin, onion powder, oregano, garlic powder, and paprika. Close and lock the lid and ensure the pressure valve is sealed, then select High Pressure and set the time for 20 minutes.
3. Once the cook time is complete, let the pressure release naturally, about 15 minutes.
4. Once all the pressure has released, carefully unlock and remove the lid. Taste and season with salt and more oil or seasonings if you like.
5. Preparation tip: If you forget to soak your chickpeas overnight, you can quick soak them in the pressure cooker: In your electric pressure cooker's cooking pot, combine the chickpeas with plenty of water (3 to 4 cups). Close and lock the lid and ensure the pressure valve is sealed, then select High Pressure and set the time for 8 minutes. Once the cook time is complete, let the pressure release naturally, about 20 minutes.
6. Ingredient tip: If you can't find ground chipotle pepper in the spice section of your grocery store, substitute 1 teaspoon chili powder plus 1 more teaspoon smoked paprika.

Nutritional Facts Per Serving:
- Calories: 280;
- Total fat: 7g;
- Protein: 13g;
- Sodium: 168mg;
- Fiber: 12g

Cinnamon Chickpeas

Serves: 4 to 6

Ingredients:
- 1 cup dried chickpeas, soaked in water overnight or quick soaked for 8 minutes on High Pressure (see tip in the recipe for Chipotle Chickpeas)
- 2 cups water
- 2 teaspoons ground cinnamon, plus more as needed
- ½ teaspoon ground nutmeg (optional)
- 1 tablespoon coconut oil
- 2 to 4 tablespoons unrefined sugar or brown sugar, plus more as needed

Directions:
1. Drain and rinse the chickpeas, then put them in your electric pressure cooker's cooking pot.
2. Add the water, cinnamon, and nutmeg (if using). Close and lock the lid and ensure the pressure valve is sealed, then select High Pressure and set the time for 30 minutes.
3. Once the cook time is complete, let the pressure release naturally, about 15 minutes.
4. Once all the pressure has released, carefully unlock and remove the lid. Drain any excess water from the chickpeas and add them back to the pot.
5. Stir in the coconut oil and sugar. Taste and add more cinnamon, if desired. Select Sauté and cook for about 5 minutes, stirring the chickpeas occasionally, until there's no liquid left and the sugar has melted onto the chickpeas. Transfer to a bowl and toss with additional sugar if you want to add a crunchy texture.
6. Variation tip: Squeeze fresh lime or lemon juice over these for a taste sensation.

Nutritional Facts Per Serving:
- Calories: 253;
- Total fat: 7g;
- Protein: 11g;
- Sodium: 9mg;
- Fiber: 10g

SOUPS, STEWS & CHILIS

Veggie Noodle Soup

Serves: 4 TO 6

Ingredients:
- 4 celery stalks, chopped into bite-size pieces
- 4 carrots, chopped into bite-size pieces
- 2 sweet potatoes, peeled and chopped into bite-size pieces
- 1 sweet onion, chopped into bite-size pieces
- 1 cup broccoli florets
- 1 tomato, diced
- 2 garlic cloves, minced
- 1 bay leaf
- 1 teaspoon dried oregano
- 1 teaspoon dried thyme
- 1 teaspoon dried basil
- 1 to 2 teaspoons salt
- Pinch freshly ground black pepper
- 1 cup dried pasta (I prefer a small pasta shape)
- 4 cups DIY Vegetable Stock, or store-bought stock, plus more as needed
- 1 to 1½ cups water, plus more as needed
- Chopped fresh parsley, for garnishing (optional)
- Lemon zest, for garnishing (optional)
- Crackers, for serving (optional)

Directions:
1. In your Instant Pot®, combine the celery, carrots, sweet potatoes, onion, broccoli, tomato, garlic, bay leaf, oregano, thyme, basil, salt, pepper, pasta, stock, and water, making sure all the good stuff is submerged (add more water or stock, if needed). Lock the lid and turn the steam release handle to Sealing. Using the Manual function, set the cooker to High Pressure for 4 minutes (3 minutes at sea level).
2. When the cook time is complete, let the pressure release naturally for 5 minutes; quick release any remaining pressure.
3. Carefully remove the lid and stir the soup. Remove and discard the bay leaf and enjoy garnished as desired!

Nutritional Facts Per Serving:
- Calories: 197;
- Total fat: 3g;
- Saturated fat: 2g;
- Sodium: 754mg;
- Carbs: 43g;
- Fiber: 6g;
- Protein: 6g

Carrot Ginger Soup

Serves: 2 TO 3

Ingredients:
- 7 carrots, chopped
- 1-inch piece fresh ginger, peeled and chopped
- ½ sweet onion, chopped
- 1¼ cups DIY Vegetable Stock, or store-bought stock
- ½ teaspoon salt, plus more as needed
- ½ teaspoon sweet paprika
- Freshly ground black pepper
- Cashew Sour Cream, for garnishing (optional)
- Fresh herbs, for garnishing (optional)

Directions:
1. In your Instant Pot®, combine the carrots, ginger, onion, stock, salt, and paprika. Season to taste with pepper. Lock the lid and turn the steam release handle to Sealing. Using the Manual function, set the cooker to High Pressure for 4 minutes (3 minutes at sea level).
2. When the cook time is complete, let the pressure release naturally for 5 minutes; quick release any remaining pressure.
3. Carefully remove the lid. Using an immersion blender, blend the soup until completely smooth. Taste and season with more salt and pepper, as needed. Serve with garnishes of choice.

Nutritional Facts Per Serving:
- Calories: 112;
- Total fat: 1g;
- Saturated fat: 1g;
- Sodium: 743mg;
- Carbs: 26g;
- Fiber: 6g;
- Protein: 2g

Creamy Tomato Basil Soup

Serves: 4 TO 6

Ingredients:
- 2 tablespoons vegan butter
- 1 small sweet onion, chopped
- 2 garlic cloves, minced
- 1 large carrot, chopped
- 1 celery stalk, chopped
- 3 cups DIY Vegetable Stock, or store-bought stock
- 3 pounds tomatoes, quartered
- ¼ cup fresh basil, chopped, plus more for garnishing
- ¼ cup nutritional yeast
- Salt
- Freshly ground black pepper
- ½ to 1 cup nondairy milk (I like cashew or coconut for this)

Directions:
1. On your Instant Pot®, select Sauté Low. When the display reads "Hot," add the butter to melt. Add the onion and garlic. Sauté for 3 to 4 minutes, stirring frequently. Add the carrot and celery and cook for 1 to 2 minutes more. Continue to stir frequently so nothing sticks.
2. Stir in the stock (now is your chance to reincorporate any veggies stuck to the bottom).
3. Add the tomatoes, basil, yeast, and a pinch or two of salt. Stir one last time. Lock the lid and turn the steam release handle to Sealing. Using the Manual function, set the cooker to High Pressure for 5 minutes (4 minutes at sea level).
4. When the cook time is complete, let the pressure release naturally for 5 to 10 minutes; quick release any remaining pressure.
5. Carefully remove the lid. Using an immersion blender, blend the soup to your preferred consistency. Stir in the milk. Taste and season with salt and pepper, as needed. Garnish with the remaining fresh basil.

Nutritional Facts Per Serving:
- Calories: 186;
- Total fat: 9g;
- Saturated fat: 3g;
- Sodium: 510mg;
- Carbs: 25g;
- Fiber: 8g;
- Protein: 9g

Cream Of Mushroom Soup

Serves: 4 TO 6

Ingredients:
- 2 tablespoons vegan butter
- 1 small sweet onion, chopped
- 1½ pounds white button mushrooms, sliced
- 2 garlic cloves, minced
- 2 teaspoons dried thyme
- 1 teaspoon sea salt
- 1¾ cups DIY Vegetable Stock, or store-bought stock
- ½ cup silken tofu
- Chopped fresh thyme, for garnishing (optional)

Directions:
1. On your Instant Pot®, select Sauté Low. When the display reads "Hot," add the butter to melt. Add the onion. Sauté for 1 to 2 minutes. Add the mushrooms, garlic, dried thyme, and salt. Cook for 2 minutes more and then turn off the Instant Pot®.
2. Stir in the stock. Lock the lid and turn the steam release handle to Sealing. Using the Manual function, set the cooker to High pressure for 6 minutes (5 minutes at sea level).
3. While the soup cooks, place the tofu in a food processor or blender and process until smooth. Set aside.
4. When the cook time is complete, let the pressure release naturally for 10 minutes; quick release any remaining pressure.
5. Carefully remove the lid. Using an immersion blender, blend the soup until completely creamy. Stir in the tofu, garnish as desired, and it's ready!
6. INGREDIENT TIP: Don't waste the rest of that tofu! Simply seal it tightly in a food storage bag and freeze, then add it to your next tofu scramble.

Nutritional Facts Per Serving:
- Calories: 111;
- Total fat: 8g;
- Saturated fat: 3g;
- Sodium: 629mg;
- Carbs: 10g;
- Fiber: 2g;
- Protein: 7g

Split Pea Soup

Serves: 4 TO 6

Ingredients:
- 1 tablespoon roasted walnut oil
- 2 carrots, diced
- 1 celery stalk, diced
- 1 teaspoon dried thyme
- 1 teaspoon smoked paprika
- 1 bay leaf
- ½ to 1 teaspoon salt, plus more as needed
- 2 garlic cloves, minced
- 1 cup green split peas
- 2½ cups DIY Vegetable Stock, or store-bought stock
- Freshly ground black pepper

Directions:
1. 1. On your Instant Pot®, select Sauté Low. When the display reads "Hot," add the oil and heat until it shimmers. Add the carrots, celery, thyme, paprika, bay leaf, and salt. Cook for 2 to 3 minutes, stirring frequently, until fragrant. Turn off the Instant Pot® and add the garlic. Cook for 30 seconds.
2. 2. Stir in the split peas and stock. Lock the lid and turn the steam release handle to Sealing. Using the Manual function, set the cooker to High Pressure for 18 minutes (15 minutes at sea level).
3. 3. When the cook time is complete, let the Instant Pot® go into Keep Warm mode and let the pressure release naturally for 15 minutes; quick release any remaining pressure.
4. 4. Carefully remove the lid, and remove and discard the bay leaf. Taste, and season with salt and pepper, as needed.
5. INGREDIENT TIP: Both green peas and green split peas are seeds from the same plant, the Pisum sativum. The difference is that the split pea is peeled and dried, which causes it to split.

Nutritional Facts Per Serving:
- Calories: 224;
- Total fat: 5g;
- Saturated fat: 2g;
- Sodium: 743mg;
- Carbs: 35g;
- Fiber: 14g;
- Protein: 13g

Potato Leek Soup

Serves: 4

Ingredients:
- 3 tablespoons vegan butter
- 2 large leeks, white and very light green parts only, cleaned well, chopped
- 2 garlic cloves, minced
- 4 cups DIY Vegetable Stock, or store-bought stock
- 1 pound Yukon Gold potatoes, cubed
- 1 bay leaf
- ½ teaspoon salt, plus more as needed
- ⅔ cup soy milk
- ⅓ cup extra-virgin olive oil
- Freshly ground white pepper

Directions:
1. On your Instant Pot®, select Sauté Low. When the display reads "Hot," add the butter and leeks. Cook for about 2 to 3 minutes until soft, stirring occasionally. Add the garlic. Cook for 30 to 45 seconds, stirring frequently, until fragrant.
2. Pour in the stock and add the potatoes, bay leaf, and salt. Stir to combine. Lock the lid and turn the steam release handle to Sealing. Using the Manual function, set the cooker to High Pressure for 5 minutes (4 minutes at sea level).
3. When the cook time is complete, let the pressure release naturally for 15 minutes; quick release any remaining pressure.
4. While waiting for the pressure to release, in a blender, combine the soy milk and olive oil. Blend until combined, about 1 minute. This is an easy dairy-free substitute for heavy cream.
5. Carefully remove the lid, remove and discard the bay leaf, and stir in the "cream." Using an immersion blender, purée the soup until smooth. Taste and season with salt and pepper, as desired.
6. INGREDIENT TIP: If you're not familiar with leeks, the most important thing to know is that you have to rinse them very well—they're grown in sandy soil, which easily collects between the layers.

Nutritional Facts Per Serving:
- Calories: 360;
- Total fat: 28g;
- Saturated fat: 6g;
- Sodium: 632mg;
- Carbs: 29g;
- Fiber: 4g;
- Protein: 4g

Cozy Wild Rice Soup

Serves: 4 TO 6

Ingredients:
- 8 tablespoons vegan butter, divided
- 5 carrots, sliced, with thicker end cut into half-moons
- 5 celery stalks, sliced
- 1 small sweet onion, diced
- 4 garlic cloves, minced
- 8 ounces baby bella mushrooms, sliced
- 2 bay leaves
- ½ teaspoon paprika
- ½ teaspoon dried thyme
- ½ teaspoon salt, plus more as needed
- 4 cups DIY Vegetable Stock, or store-bought stock
- 1 cup wild rice
- ½ cup all-purpose flour
- 1 cup nondairy milk
- Freshly ground black pepper

Directions:
1. On your Instant Pot®, select Sauté Low. When the display reads "Hot," add 2 tablespoons of butter to melt. Add the carrots, celery, onion, garlic, mushrooms, bay leaves, paprika, thyme, and salt. Cook for 2 to 3 minutes, just until fragrant. Turn off the Instant Pot®.
2. Stir in the stock and wild rice. Lock the lid and turn the steam release handle to Sealing. Using the Manual function, set the cooker to High Pressure for 35 minutes (30 minutes at sea level).
3. When there are just a few minutes of cook time remaining, in a small pan over medium-low heat on your stovetop, melt the remaining 6 tablespoons of butter. Whisk in the flour and cook for 3 to 4 minutes. Whisk in the milk, getting rid of any lumps to finish the roux.
4. When the cook time is complete, quick release the pressure.
5. Carefully remove the lid, and remove and discard the bay leaves. Select Sauté Low again. Stir in the roux and let warm through and thicken. Taste and season with salt and pepper, as needed.
6. TECHNIQUE TIP: You may be wondering why the roux goes in at the end, when you're used to those steps being first. It's because thickeners such as flour and cornstarch don't work the same in the Instant Pot® as they do on the stovetop. Add them at the end, and they'll work just the way they're meant to!
7. INGREDIENT TIP: Wild rice (which isn't even actually rice . . . it's grass!) can be found in most health stores and in many grocery stores. A lot of stores don't stock it with the regular rice, but rather with the specialty grains.

Nutritional Facts Per Serving:
- Calories: 480;
- Total fat: 26g;
- Saturated fat: 6g;
- Sodium: 754mg;
- Carbs: 57g;
- Fiber: 6g;
- Protein: 10g

Curried Squash Soup

Serves: 4 TO 6

Ingredients:
- 1 tablespoon olive oil
- 1 onion, chopped
- 2 garlic cloves, chopped
- 1 tablespoon curry powder
- 1 (2- to 3-pound) butternut squash, peeled and cubed
- 4 cups DIY Vegetable Stock, or store-bought stock
- 1 teaspoon salt
- 1 (14-ounce) can lite coconut milk

Directions:
1. On your Instant Pot®, select Sauté Low. When the display reads "Hot," add the oil and heat until it shimmers. Add the onion. Cook for 3 to 4 minutes, stirring frequently. Turn off the Instant Pot® and add the garlic and curry powder. Cook for 1 minute, stirring. It should start smelling delicious right about now!
2. Add the squash, stock, and salt. Lock the lid and turn the steam release handle to Sealing. Using the Manual function, set the cooker to High Pressure for 30 minutes (25 minutes at sea level).
3. When the cook time is complete, quick release the pressure.
4. Carefully remove the lid. Using an immersion blender, blend the soup until completely smooth. Stir in the coconut milk, saving a little bit for topping when served.

Nutritional Facts Per Serving:
- Calories: 267;
- Total fat: 11g;
- Saturated fat: 7g;
- Sodium: 843mg;
- Carbs: 50g;
- Fiber: 8g;
- Protein: 5g

Smoky White Bean Soup

Serves: 4 TO 6

Ingredients:
- 1 cup dried great northern white beans, rinsed
- 1 small to medium tomato, diced
- ¼ cup raw millet
- 1 cube vegetable or "not chicken" bouillon
- 1 to 1½ teaspoons smoked paprika, plus more as needed
- 1 teaspoon salt, plus more as needed
- 3½ to 4 cups water, plus more as needed
- 1 (14-ounce) can lite coconut milk
- 1 cup frozen sweet corn

Directions:
1. In your Instant Pot®, stir together the beans, tomato, millet, bouillon cube, paprika, salt, water, and coconut milk. Lock the lid and turn the steam release handle to Sealing. Using the Manual function, set the cooker to High Pressure for 32 minutes (27 minutes at sea level).
2. When the cook time is complete, turn off the Instant Pot® (don't let it go into Keep Warm mode) and let the pressure release naturally for 10 minutes; quick release any remaining pressure.
3. Carefully remove the lid and stir in the corn. Taste and adjust the seasonings, as needed.
4. MAKE-AHEAD TIP: This soup thickens as it cools, so if you're saving some for leftovers, have additional water or nondairy milk on hand when you're ready to reheat.

Nutritional Facts Per Serving:
- Calories: 183;
- Total fat: 7g;
- Saturated fat: 6g;
- Sodium: 864mg;
- Carbs: 27g;
- Fiber: 4g;
- Protein: 6g

Minestrone Soup

Serves: 4 TO 6

Ingredients:
- 2 tablespoons olive oil
- 2 celery stalks, sliced
- 1 sweet onion, diced
- 1 large carrot, sliced, with thicker end cut into half-moons
- 2 garlic cloves, minced
- 1 teaspoon dried oregano
- 1 teaspoon dried basil
- ½ to 1 teaspoon salt, plus more as needed
- 1 bay leaf
- 1 zucchini, roughly diced
- 1 (28-ounce) can diced tomatoes
- 1 (16-ounce) can kidney beans, drained and rinsed
- 1 cup small dried pasta
- 6 cups DIY Vegetable Stock, or store-bought stock
- 2 to 3 cups fresh baby spinach
- Freshly ground black pepper

Directions:
1. On your Instant Pot®, select Sauté Low. When the display reads "Hot," add the oil, celery, onion, and carrot. Cook for 2 to 3 minutes, stirring frequently. Add the garlic and cook for another minute or so, stirring frequently. Turn off the Instant Pot® and add the oregano, basil, salt, and bay leaf. Stir and let sit for 30 seconds to 1 minute.
2. Add the zucchini, tomatoes, kidney beans, pasta, and stock. Lock the lid and turn the steam release handle to Sealing. Using the Manual function, set the cooker to High Pressure for 4 minutes (3 minutes at sea level).
3. When the cook time is complete, quick release the pressure.
4. Carefully remove the lid, and remove and discard the bay leaf. Stir in the spinach and let it get all nice and wilty. Taste and season with more salt, as needed, and pepper. Serve hot.

Nutritional Facts Per Serving:
- Calories: 332;
- Total fat: 12g;
- Saturated fat: 4g;
- Sodium: 654mg;
- Carbs: 54g;
- Fiber: 12g;
- Protein: 13g

Veggie Noodle Soup

Serves: 4

Ingredients:
- Celery – 4 stalks, chopped into bite-sized pieces
- Carrots – 4, chopped into bite-sized pieces
- Sweet potatoes – 2, peeled and chopped
- Sweet onion – 1, chopped
- Broccoli florets – 1 cup
- Tomato – 1, diced
- Garlic – 2 cloves, minced
- Bay leaf – 1
- Dried oregano – 1 tsp.
- Dried thyme – 1 tsp.
- Dried basil – 1 tsp.
- Salt – 1 to 2 tsp.
- Ground black pepper
- Dried pasta – 1 cup
- Vegetable stock – 4 cups, plus more as needed
- Water – 1 to ½ cups, plus more as needed
- Chopped fresh parsley, for garnish
- Lemon zest for garnish
- Crackers, for serving

Directions:
1. In the Instant Pot, combine the water, stock, pasta, salt, pepper, basil, thyme, oregano, bay leaf, garlic, tomato, broccoli, onion, sweet potatoes, carrots, and celery.
2. Cover the Instant Pot.
3. Cook on High for 3 minutes.
4. Do a natural release and then a quick release.
5. Remove the lid and stir the soup.
6. Discard the bay leaf, garnish and serve.

Nutritional Facts Per Serving:
- Calories: 197
- Fat: 3g
- Carb: 43g
- Protein: 6g

Carrot Ginger Soup

Serves: 2

Ingredients:
- Carrots – 7 chopped
- Fresh ginger – 1-inch, peeled and chopped
- Sweet onion – ½, chopped
- Vegetable stock – 1 ¼ cups
- Salt – ½ tsp.
- Sweet paprika – ½ tsp.
- Ground black pepper
- Cashew sour cream for garnish
- Fresh herbs for garnish

Directions:
1. In the Instant Pot, combine the paprika, salt, stock, onion, ginger, and carrots. Season with pepper.
2. Cover the Instant Pot.
3. Cook on High for 3 minutes.
4. Do a natural release and then a quick release.
5. Open and blend with a hand mixer until smooth.
6. Garnish and serve.

Nutritional Facts Per Serving:
- Calories: 112
- Fat: 1g
- Carb: 26g
- Protein: 2g

Creamy Tomato Basil Soup

Serves: 4

Ingredients:
- Vegan butter – 2 Tbsp.
- Small sweet onion – 1, chopped
- Garlic – 2 cloves, minced
- Carrot – 1, chopped
- Celery – 1 stalk, chopped
- Vegetable stock – 3 cups
- Tomatoes – 3 pounds, quartered
- Fresh basil – ¼ cup, plus more for garnishing
- Nutritional yeast – ¼ cup
- Salt and ground black pepper
- Nondairy milk – ½ to 1 cup

Directions:
1. Press Sauté on the Instant Pot, add butter and melt.
2. Add the garlic and onion and stir-fry for 3 to 4 minutes.
3. Add celery and carrot and cook 2 minutes more. Stir continuously.
4. Add the stock and deglaze the pot.
5. Add salt, yeast, basil, and tomatoes. Stir to mix.
6. Cover the Instant Pot.
7. Cook on High for 4 minutes.
8. Do a natural release than a quick release.
9. Open and blend with a hand mixer until smooth.
10. Stir in milk. Taste and adjust seasoning.
11. Garnish and serve.

Nutritional Facts Per Serving:
- Calories: 186
- Fat: 9g
- Carb: 25g
- Protein: 9g

Cream Of Mushroom Soup

Serves: 4

Ingredients:
- Vegan butter – 2 Tbsp.
- Small sweet onion – 1, chopped
- White button mushrooms – 1 ½ pound, sliced
- Garlic – 2 cloves, minced
- Dried thyme – 2 tsp.
- Sea salt -1 tsp.
- Vegetable stock – 1 ¾ cup
- Silken tofu – ½ cup
- Chopped fresh thyme for garnishing

Directions:
1. Press Sauté on the Instant Pot. Melt the butter and add the onion. Stir-fry for 2 minutes. Add the salt, dried thyme, garlic, and mushrooms. Stir-fry for 2 minutes more and press Cancel.
2. Stir in the stock. Cover the Instant Pot.
3. Cook on High for 5 minutes.
4. Meanwhile, process the tofu in a food processor until smooth. Set aside.
5. Do a natural release, then quick release.
6. Open and blend with a hand mixer until smooth.
7. Garnish and serve.

Nutritional Facts Per Serving:
- Calories: 111
- Fat: 8g
- Carb: 10g
- Protein: 7g

Split Pea Soup

Serves: 4

Ingredients:
- Roasted walnut oil – 1 Tbsp.
- Carrots – 2, diced
- Celery – 1 stalk, diced
- Dried thyme – 1 tsp.
- Smoked paprika – 1 tsp.
- Bay leaf – 1
- Salt – ½ to 1 tsp. plus more as needed
- Garlic – 2 cloves, minced
- Green split peas – 1 cup
- Vegetable stock – 2 ½ cups
- Ground black pepper

Directions:
1. Press Sauté on the Instant Pot. Add oil.
2. Add salt, bay leaf, paprika, thyme, celery, and carrots. Stir-fry for 3 minutes, then add garlic and cook for 30 seconds more.
3. Stir in the split peas and stock. Cover the Instant Pot.
4. Cook on High for 15 minutes.
5. Do a natural release then quick release.
6. Open and discard the bay leaf.
7. Taste and adjust seasoning and serve.

Nutritional Facts Per Serving:
- Calories: 224
- Fat: 5g
- Carb: 35g
- Protein: 13g

Potato Leek Soup

Serves: 4

Ingredients:
- Vegan butter – 3 Tbsp.
- Large leeks – 2, white and light green parts only, chopped
- Garlic – 2 cloves, minced
- Vegetable stock – 4 cups
- Yukon Gold potatoes – 1 pound, cubed
- Bay leaf - 1
- Salt – ½ tsp. plus more as needed
- Soy milk – 2/3 cup
- Extra-virgin olive oil – 1/3 cup
- Ground black pepper

Directions:
1. Press Sauté on the Instant Pot.
2. Add butter and leeks. Stir-fry for 3 minutes.
3. Add the garlic.
4. Cook for 30 seconds more.
5. Add stock, salt, bay leaf, and potatoes. Mix.
6. Cover the Instant Pot.
7. Cook on High for 4 minutes.
8. Do a natural release and then quick release.
9. Meanwhile, in a blender, combine olive oil and soymilk. Blend until smooth.
10. Open and discard the bay leaf. Stir in the soymilk-olive oil mixture.
11. Blend with a hand mixer until smooth.
12. Taste and adjust seasoning. Serve.

Nutritional Facts Per Serving:
- Calories: 360
- Fat: 28g
- Carb: 29g
- Protein: 4g

Wild Rice Soup

Serves: 4

Ingredients:
- Vegan butter – 8 Tbsp. divided
- Carrots – 5, sliced
- Celery stalks – 5, diced
- Small sweet onion – 1, diced
- Garlic – 4 cloves, minced
- Baby Bella mushrooms – 8 ounces, sliced
- Bay leaves – 2
- Paprika – ½ tsp.
- Dried thyme – ½ tsp.
- Salt – ½ tsp. plus more as needed
- Vegetable stock – 4 cups
- Wild rice – 1 cup
- All-purpose flour – ½ cup
- Nondairy milk – 1 cup
- Ground black pepper

Directions:
1. Press Sauté on the Instant Pot and add 2 tbsp. butter.
2. Add the salt, thyme, paprika, bay leaves, mushrooms, garlic, onion, celery, and carrots. Cook for 2 to 3 minutes.
3. Stir in the wild rice and stock. Cover the Instant Pot.
4. Cook on High for 30 minutes.
5. Heat the remaining 6 tbsp. of butter in a saucepan. Add flour and cook for 3 to 4 minutes. Whisk in the milk and mix well.
6. Do a quick release when the cooking is complete.
7. Open and discard the bay leaves.
8. Press Sauté, stir in the roux. Mix and thicken.
9. Taste and adjust seasoning and serve.

Nutritional Facts Per Serving:
- Calories: 480
- Fat: 26g
- Carb: 57g
- Protein: 10g

Curried Squash Soup

Serves: 4

Ingredients:
- Olive oil - 1 Tbsp.
- Onion – 1, chopped
- Garlic – 2 cloves, chopped
- Curry powder – 1 Tbsp.
- Butternut squash – 1 (2 to 3-pound), cubed
- Vegetable stock – 4 cups
- Salt – 1 tsp.
- Lite coconut milk – 1 (14-ounce) can

Directions:
1. Press Sauté on the Instant Pot. Add oil.
2. Add onion and stir-fry for 3 to 4 minutes. Add curry powder and garlic and cook for 1 minute.
3. Add the stock, squash, and salt. Cover the Instant Pot.
4. Cook on High for 25 minutes.
5. Do a quick release.
6. Open and blend with a hand mixer.
7. Stir in the coconut milk and serve.

Nutritional Facts Per Serving:
- Calories: 267
- Fat: 11g
- Carb: 50g
- Protein: 5g

Smoky White Bean Soup

Serves: 4

Ingredients:
- Dried great northern white bean – 1 cup, rinsed
- Tomato – 1, diced
- Raw millet – ¼ cup
- Vegetable cube – 1
- Smoked paprika – 1 to 1 ½ tsp.
- Salt -1 tsp.
- Water – 4 cups plus more as needed
- Lite coconut milk – 1 (14-ounce) can
- Frozen sweet corn – 1 cup

Directions:
1. In the Instant Pot, stir together the coconut milk, water, salt, paprika, bouillon cube, millet, tomato, and beans.
2. Cover and cook on High for 27 minutes.
3. Do a natural release.
4. Open and stir in the corn.
5. Taste and adjust the seasoning and serve.

Nutritional Facts Per Serving:
- Calories: 183
- Fat: 7g
- Carb: 27g
- Protein: 6g

Minestrone Soup

Serves: 4

Ingredients:
- Olive oil – 2 Tbsp.
- Celery stalks – 2, sliced
- Sweet onion – 1, diced
- Large carrot – 1, sliced
- Garlic – 2 cloves, minced
- Dried oregano – 1 tsp.
- Dried basil – 1 tsp.
- Salt – ½ tsp. to 1 tsp. plus more as needed
- Bay leaf – 1
- Zucchini – 1, diced
- Diced tomatoes – 1 (28-ounce) can
- Kidney beans – 1 (16-ounce) can, drained and rinsed
- Dried pasta – 1 cup
- Vegetable stock – 6 cups
- Fresh baby spinach – 2 to 3 cups
- Ground black pepper

Directions:
1. Press Sauté on your Instant Pot.
2. Add oil, carrot, onion, and celery. Stir-fry for 2 to 3 minutes.
3. Now add garlic and stir-fry for 1 minute.
4. Add bay leaf, salt, basil, and oregano. Stir and let sit for 30 seconds.
5. Add the stock, pasta, kidney beans, tomatoes, and zucchini.
6. Cover the Instant Pot.
7. Cook on High for 3 minutes.
8. Do a quick release.
9. Open and discard the bay leaf. Stir in spinach.
10. Taste and adjust seasoning.
11. Serve.

Nutritional Facts Per Serving:
- Calories: 332
- Fat: 12g
- Carb: 54g
- Protein: 13g

Lasagna Soup

Serves: 4

Ingredients:
- Olive oil – 2 Tbsp.
- Medium onion – 1, diced
- Garlic - 1 clove, diced
- Dried oregano – 2 tsp.
- Dried rosemary – 1 tsp.
- Red pepper flakes – ½ to ¾ tsp.
- Tomatoes – 2, chopped
- Vegetable cube – 1
- Bay leaf – 1
- Lasagna noodles – 10, broken into smaller pieces
- Red sauce – ½ to 2/3 cup
- Water – 6 cups
- Salt and black pepper
- Fresh basil for garnishing
- Vegan mozzarella cheese – for garnishing, shredded

Directions:
1. Press Sauté on the Instant Pot. Add oil and onion.
2. Stir-fry for 3 minutes. Add garlic and turn off the heat.
3. Stir-fry for a few seconds.
4. Add the water, red sauce, noodle, bay leaf, bouillon cube, tomatoes, salt, red pepper flakes, rosemary, and oregano. Submerge the noodles and cover the lid.
5. Cook 3 minutes on High.
6. Do a natural release, then quick release.
7. Open and discard the bay leaf. Taste and adjust seasoning.
8. Serve.

Nutritional Facts Per Serving:
- Calories: 311
- Fat: 9g
- Carb: 50g
- Protein: 10g

VEGETABLE

Mashed Potatoes

Serves: 4 to 6

Ingredients:
- 4 to 6 medium russet potatoes, scrubbed or peeled and uniformly chopped (about 5 cups)
- 1 cup unsalted vegetable broth or water
- Salt
- 2 to 4 tablespoons olive oil, coconut oil, or vegan margarine
- 2 to 4 tablespoons unsweetened nondairy milk
- ½ teaspoon garlic powder (optional)

Directions:
1. In your electric pressure cooker's cooking pot, combine the potatoes, vegetable broth, and a pinch of salt. Close and lock the lid and ensure the pressure valve is sealed, then select High Pressure and set the time for 5 minutes.
2. Once the cook time is complete, quick release the pressure, being careful not to get your fingers or face near the steam release.
3. Once all the pressure has released, carefully unlock and remove the lid. Using oven mitts, lift out the pot.
4. Add the olive oil, milk, and garlic powder (if using) to the pot. Using a potato masher, mash the potatoes. Alternatively, use an immersion blender right in the pot to purée the potatoes to the texture you want. Taste and season with more salt, if needed.Ingredient tip: Using vegetable broth to cook the potatoes adds more flavor, but use water if you prefer.

Nutritional Facts Per Serving:
- Calories: 233;
- Total fat: 7g;
- Protein: 4g;
- Sodium: 162mg;
- Fiber: 4g

Potato Salad

Serves: 4 to 6

Ingredients:
- 4 to 6 medium russet potatoes, scrubbed and cut in large uniform cubes (4 to 5 cups)
- ½ cup unsweetened nondairy yogurt
- 2 teaspoons Dijon mustard
- 1½ teaspoons apple cider vinegar
- ½ teaspoon onion powder (optional)
- ¼ teaspoon salt
- 3 or 4 celery stalks, chopped
- 2 scallions, chopped
- Freshly ground black pepper

Directions:
1. Put the potatoes in a steaming basket.
2. Put a trivet in your electric pressure cooker's cooking pot, pour in a cup or two of water, and set the steaming basket on the trivet. (Alternatively, you can cook the potatoes right in the water, though they will end up quite a bit softer.) Close and lock the lid and ensure the pressure valve is sealed, then select High Pressure and set the time for 6 minutes.
3. Once the cook time is complete, let the pressure release naturally, about 10 minutes.
4. Meanwhile, in a large bowl, stir together the yogurt, mustard, vinegar, onion powder (if using), and salt. Add the celery and scallions and stir to combine.
5. Once all the pressure has released, carefully unlock and remove the lid. Using oven mitts, carefully lift the steaming basket out of the pot (or drain the potatoes if you cooked them directly in the water). Let the potatoes cool for a few minutes, then stir them into the bowl with the vegetables and dressing. Taste and season with pepper.
6. Variation tip: Add a large handful of chopped fresh parsley and/or spinach to boost the nutritional content of your salad.

Nutritional Facts Per Serving:
- Calories: 201;
- Total fat: 1g;
- Protein: 5g;
- Sodium: 52mg;
- Fiber: 5g

Spicy Potato Bites With Avocado Dip

Serves: 4

Ingredients:
- 4 to 6 medium russet potatoes, scrubbed and cut in large uniform cubes (4 to 5 cups)
- 1 avocado, peeled and pitted
- 2 tablespoons freshly squeezed lime juice
- 2 teaspoons onion powder, divided
- 1 teaspoon garlic powder, divided
- Pinch salt
- 1 to 2 tablespoons water, if needed
- 1 tablespoon olive oil
- ½ teaspoon smoked paprika
- ¼ teaspoon ground chipotle pepper

Directions:
1. Put the potatoes in a steaming basket.
2. Put a trivet in your electric pressure cooker's cooking pot, pour in a cup or two of water, and set the steaming basket on top. Close and lock the lid and ensure the pressure valve is sealed. Select High Pressure and set the time for 6 minutes.
3. Once the cook time is complete, let the pressure release naturally, about 10 minutes.
4. In a blender, combine the avocado, lime juice, 1 teaspoon of onion powder, ½ teaspoon of garlic powder, and the salt. Purée, adding the water if needed to achieve your preferred consistency. Transfer to a serving bowl.
5. Once all the pressure has released, carefully unlock and remove the lid. Using oven mitts, lift the steaming basket out of the pot.
6. Put the empty pot back into the pressure cooker and select Sauté. Return the potatoes to the pot and add the olive oil, remaining 1 teaspoon of onion powder, remaining ½ teaspoon of garlic powder, paprika, and chipotle pepper. Cook for about 2 minutes, stirring occasionally, until any liquid has evaporated. Serve the potatoes with the avocado dipping sauce.

Nutritional Facts Per Serving:
- Calories: 205;
- Total fat: 6g;
- Protein: 4g;
- Sodium: 153mg;
- Fiber: 5g

Lemon-Dill Baby Potatoes

Serves: 4

Ingredients:
- 2 pounds baby potatoes, scrubbed
- 2 tablespoons olive oil
- 2 tablespoons freshly squeezed lemon juice
- 1 teaspoon dried dill
- 2 tablespoons nutritional yeast (optional)
- Salt

Directions:
1. 1.Pour a cup or two of water into your electric pressure cooker's cooking pot and add the potatoes. Close and lock the lid and ensure the pressure valve is sealed, then select High Pressure and set the time for 10 minutes.
2. 2.Once the cook time is complete, let the pressure release naturally, about 10 minutes.
3. 3.Once all the pressure has released, carefully unlock and remove the lid. Drain the potatoes.
4. 4.In a small bowl, whisk together the olive oil, lemon juice, dill, and nutritional yeast (if using). Add to the pot and toss the potatoes to coat.
5. Preparation tip: If you want to infuse more flavor into your potatoes, pour the water in the pot, toss the potatoes in a large bowl with the dressing, and steam them in a dish above the water.

Nutritional Facts Per Serving:
- Calories: 218;
- Total fat: 7g;
- Protein: 6g;
- Sodium: 80mg;
- Fiber: 4g

Sweet Potato Breakfast Bowls

Serves: 2

Ingredients:
- 1 sweet potato, peeled and chopped
- 1 apple or pear, cored and quartered
- ½ cup nondairy milk, plus more as needed
- 2 tablespoons nut or seed butter (almond, cashew, sunflower)
- ¼ teaspoon ground cinnamon (optional)
- Pinch ground nutmeg (optional)
- Unrefined sugar or pure maple syrup, for serving (optional)

Directions:
1. In a heat-proof dish that fits inside your electric pressure cooker's cooking pot, combine the sweet potato and apple.
2. Put a trivet in the pot, pour in a cup or two of water, and set the dish on the trivet. If it's a tight fit, use a foil sling or silicone helper handles to lower the dish onto the trivet (see here). Close and lock the lid and ensure the pressure valve is sealed, then select High Pressure and set the time for 6 minutes.
3. Once the cook time is complete, let the pressure release naturally, about 10 minutes.
4. Once all the pressure has released, carefully unlock and remove the lid. Let cool for a few minutes before carefully lifting out the dish with oven mitts or tongs. Transfer the sweet potatoes and apples to a blender.
5. Add the milk, nut butter, cinnamon (if using), and nutmeg (if using). Purée. Add more milk if needed, plus sugar or maple syrup, if you like.
6. Serving tip: Top with something crunchy, such as chopped fresh apples, slivered almonds, pumpkin seeds, or granola.

Nutritional Facts Per Serving:
- Calories: 302;
- Total fat: 13g;
- Protein: 6g;
- Sodium: 115mg;
- Fiber: 8g

Balsamic And Red Wine Mushrooms

Serves: 4

Ingredients:
- ¼ cup dry red wine
- ¼ cup water
- 2 tablespoons balsamic vinegar
- 1 tablespoon olive oil
- 1 teaspoon cornstarch or arrowroot powder
- ½ teaspoon dried basil or mixed herbs
- ¼ teaspoon salt, plus more as needed
- Freshly ground black pepper

Directions:
1. 1 pound white mushrooms, quartered
2. 1.In your electric pressure cooker's cooking pot, stir together the red wine, water, vinegar, olive oil, cornstarch, basil, and salt. Season with pepper. Add the mushrooms to the sauce. Close and lock the lid and ensure the pressure valve is sealed, then select High Pressure and set the time for 2 minutes.
3. 2.Once the cook time is complete, quick release the pressure, being careful not to get your fingers or face near the steam release.
4. 3.Once all the pressure has released, carefully unlock and remove the lid. Taste and season with more salt and pepper, if needed.

Nutritional Facts Per Serving:
- Calories: 72;
- Total fat: 3g;
- Protein: 2g;
- Sodium: 151mg;
- Fiber: 0g

Ratatouille

Serves: 4to 6

Ingredients:
- 1 onion, diced
- 4 garlic cloves, minced
- 1 to 2 teaspoons olive oil
- 1 or 2 bell peppers, any color, seeded and chopped
- 1½ tablespoons dried herbes de Provence (or any mixture of dried basil, oregano, thyme, marjoram, and rosemary)
- ½ teaspoon salt
- Freshly ground black pepper
- 1 cup water
- 3 or 4 tomatoes, diced
- 1 eggplant, cubed

Directions:
1. 1.On your electric pressure cooker, select Sauté. Add the onion, garlic, and olive oil. Cook for 4 to 5 minutes, stirring occasionally, until the onion is softened. Add the water, tomatoes, eggplant, bell peppers, and herbes de Provence. Cancel Sauté.
2. 2.Close and lock the lid and ensure the pressure valve is sealed, then select High Pressure and set the time for 6 minutes.
3. 3.Once the cook time is complete, let the pressure release naturally, about 20 minutes.
4. 4.Once all the pressure has released, carefully unlock and remove the lid. Let cool for a few minutes, then season with salt and pepper.
5. Serving tip: Serve with couscous or rice, and maybe a sprinkle of toasted pine nuts on top!

Nutritional Facts Per Serving:
- Calories: 101;
- Total fat: 2g;
- Protein: 4g;
- Sodium: 304mg;
- Fiber: 7g

Spaghetti Squash Primavera

Serves: 3 to 4

Ingredients:
- 1 spaghetti squash
- 2 or 3 garlic cloves, minced
- 1 to 2 tablespoons olive oil or vegan margarine, plus more as needed
- 1 cup peas
- 2 to 3 tablespoons nutritional yeast, plus more as needed
- Salt
- 1 cup cherry tomatoes, halved
- Freshly ground black pepper

Directions:
1. Put the spaghetti squash in your electric pressure cooker's cooking pot. (If the squash won't fit, cut it in half, scoop out the seeds with a large spoon, and stack the halves in the pot cut-side down.) Pour in a cup or two of water. Close and lock the lid and ensure the pressure valve is sealed, then select High Pressure and set the time for 10 to 15 minutes, depending on the size of your squash. (If you've cut the squash in half, set the time for 5 to 7 minutes, depending on size.)
2. Once the cook time is complete, let the pressure release naturally, about 10 minutes.
3. Once all the pressure has released, carefully unlock and remove the lid. Using tongs or a large fork and spoon, carefully lift out the squash and set it aside to cool.
4. Empty the water from the pot and return the pot to the pressure cooker. Select Sauté. Add the garlic and olive oil and cook for about 2 minutes, stirring occasionally, until the garlic is lightly browned. Add the peas and cook for 1 to 2 minutes to soften.
5. If the squash is whole, cut it in half and scoop out the seeds. Using a fork, scrape the squash flesh into strands and return them to the pot. Sprinkle the strands with the nutritional yeast and season with salt. Toss to coat in the oil.
6. Add the cherry tomatoes, plus more nutritional yeast, olive oil, salt, and pepper, if needed.
7. Variation tip: To make a delicious and protein-rich topping for this dish, pulse together some cooked chickpeas and pitted black olives in a food processor until finely chopped.

Nutritional Facts Per Serving:
- Calories: 165;
- Total fat: 6g;
- Protein: 8g;
- Sodium: 126mg;
- Fiber: 5g

Beet Marinara Sauce

Serves: 6

Ingredients:
- 1 onion, diced
- 2 garlic cloves, minced
- 1 tablespoon olive oil
- 6 to 8 carrots, peeled or scrubbed and chopped (about 5 cups)
- 2 medium beets, scrubbed and chopped (about 2 cups)
- 1 teaspoon salt, plus more as needed
- 1 cup water
- 1 tablespoon dried basil
- 2 tablespoons freshly squeezed lemon juice
- Freshly ground black pepper

Directions:
1. On your electric pressure cooker, select Sauté. Add the onion, garlic, and olive oil. Cook for 2 to 3 minutes, stirring occasionally, until the onion is softened. Add the carrots, beets, salt, and water. Cancel Sauté.
2. Close and lock the lid and ensure the pressure valve is sealed, then select High Pressure and set the time for 10 minutes.
3. Once the cook time is complete, let the pressure release naturally, about 15 minutes.
4. Once all the pressure has released, carefully unlock and remove the lid. Stir in the basil and lemon juice. Let cool for a few minutes, then purée the beets and carrots—either use an immersion blender right in the pot or transfer to a countertop blender and add more water, if needed. Taste and season with more salt and pepper, if needed.
5. Ingredient tip: If you have fresh basil, use a small handful instead of the dried for a fresh boost of flavor.

Nutritional Facts Per Serving:
- Calories: 97;
- Total fat: 3g;
- Protein: 2g;
- Sodium: 498mg;
- Fiber: 5g

Butternut Squash And Pineapple

Serves: 4

Ingredients:
- 1 butternut squash
- 4 cups chopped bok choy
- 1 scallion, chopped
- 1 to 2 teaspoons toasted sesame oil
- 10 ounces bite-size pineapple chunks (about 1½ cups)
- 1 to 2 tablespoons tamari or soy sauce

Directions:
1. Put the butternut squash in your electric pressure cooker's cooking pot. (If the squash won't fit, cut it in half lengthwise, scoop out the seeds with a large spoon, and stack the halves in the pot, cut-side down.) Pour in a cup or two of water. Close and lock the lid and ensure the pressure valve is sealed, then select High Pressure and set the time for 10 to 15 minutes, depending on the size of your squash. (If you've cut the squash in half, set the time for 5 to 7 minutes, depending on size.)
2. Once the cook time is complete, let the pressure release naturally, about 10 minutes.
3. Once all the pressure has released, carefully unlock and remove the lid. Using tongs or a large fork and spoon, carefully lift the squash out of the pot and let cool for a few minutes.
4. Empty the water from the pot and return the pot to the pressure cooker. Select Sauté. Add the bok choy, scallion, and sesame oil. Cook for 1 minute, stirring occasionally, until the vegetables are softened.
5. If the squash is whole, cut it in half lengthwise, scoop out the seeds, and remove the skin. Chop the squash into bite-size chunks and add them to the pot, along with the pineapple and tamari. Toss to combine until heated through.

Nutritional Facts Per Serving:
- Calories: 193;
- Total fat: 8g;
- Protein: 6g;
- Sodium: 259mg;
- Fiber: 5g

Red Thai Curry Cauliflower

Serves: 4 TO 6

Ingredients:
- 1 (14-ounce) can full-fat coconut milk
- ½ to 1 cup water
- 2 tablespoons red curry paste
- 1 teaspoon garlic powder
- 1 teaspoon salt, plus more as needed
- ½ teaspoon ground ginger
- ½ teaspoon onion powder
- ¼ teaspoon chili powder (Thai is great, or cayenne pepper)
- 1 bell pepper, any color, thinly sliced
- 1 small to medium head cauliflower, cut into bite-size pieces (3 to 4 cups)
- 1 (14-ounce) can diced tomatoes and liquid
- Freshly ground black pepper
- Cooked rice or other grain, for serving (optional)

Directions:
1. In your Instant Pot®, stir together the coconut milk, water, red curry paste, garlic powder, salt, ginger, onion powder, and chili powder. Add the bell pepper, cauliflower, and tomatoes, and stir again. Lock the lid and turn the steam release handle to Sealing. Using the Manual function, set the cooker to High Pressure for 2 minutes.
2. When the cook time is complete, quick release the pressure.
3. Carefully remove the lid and give the whole thing a good stir. Taste and season with more salt and pepper, as needed. Serve with rice or another grain (if using).
4. INGREDIENT TIP: Full-fat coconut milk helps make this curry rich and thick, but you can use the lighter-calorie lower-fat version, if you prefer.

Nutritional Facts Per Serving:
- Calories: 349;
- Total fat: 31g;
- Saturated fat: 26g;
- Sodium: 943mg;
- Carbs: 18g;
- Fiber: 6g;
- Protein: 5g

Polenta & Kale

Serves: 4 TO 6

Ingredients:
- 1 tablespoon olive oil
- 2 bunches kale, stemmed, leaves chopped
- 3 or 4 garlic cloves, minced
- 1 teaspoon salt, divided, plus more as needed
- 1 cup polenta
- 1 quart DIY Vegetable Stock, or store-bought stock
- 2 tablespoons nutritional yeast
- 2 to 3 tablespoons vegan butter
- Freshly ground black pepper

Directions:
1. On your Instant Pot®, select Sauté Low. When the display reads "Hot," add the oil and heat until it shimmers. Add the kale, garlic, and ½ teaspoon of salt. Cook for about 2 minutes, stirring frequently so nothing burns, until the kale is soft and the garlic is fragrant. (You can always turn off the Instant Pot® if it gets too hot.) Transfer the garlicky kale to a bowl and set aside.
2. In your Instant Pot®, combine the polenta, stock, and remaining ½ teaspoon of salt. Lock the lid and turn the steam release handle to Sealing. Using the Manual function, set the cooker to High Pressure for 20 minutes (17 minutes at sea level).
3. When the cook time is complete, let the pressure release naturally for 15 minutes; quick release any remaining pressure.
4. Carefully remove the lid and stir well (some liquid may have accumulated on top of the polenta). Add the nutritional yeast and butter along with any additional salt and pepper. Serve in bowls topped with the kale.

Nutritional Facts Per Serving:
- Calories: 329;
- Total fat: 13g;
- Saturated fat: 2g;
- Sodium: 729mg;
- Carbs: 46g;
- Fiber: 5g;
- Protein: 10g

Butternut Mac 'N' Cheese

Serves: 6

Ingredients:
- 1 cup raw cashews, soaked in water for at least 3 to 4 hours, or overnight, drained and rinsed well
- 2 cups cooked cubed butternut squash (I buy frozen cubes and thaw them in advance)
- ⅓ cup nutritional yeast
- 2 tablespoons freshly squeezed lemon juice
- 1 teaspoon Dijon mustard
- 2 to 2½ teaspoons salt
- ⅛ teaspoon ground nutmeg
- 4½ cups water, divided
- 1 (16-ounce) box pasta (I like small shells or campanelle)
- 1 cup nondairy milk, plus more as needed
- Freshly ground black pepper

Directions:
1. In a high-speed blender or food processor, combine the cashews, squash, nutritional yeast, lemon juice, mustard, salt, nutmeg, and 2 cups of water. Blend until smooth (the longer you soaked the cashews, the quicker this will be). Pour the cashew mixture into your Instant Pot®.
2. Pour the remaining 2½ cups of water into the blender and swish it around to capture any remaining cashew mixture. Add that to the Instant Pot® as well, along with the pasta. Lock the lid and turn the steam release handle to Sealing. Using the Manual function, set the cooker to Low Pressure for 2 minutes.
3. When the cook time is complete, turn off the Instant Pot® and let the pressure release naturally for 8 minutes; quick release any remaining pressure.
4. Carefully remove the lid and stir in the milk, adding as much as needed to make it nice and creamy. Taste and season with more salt and pepper, as needed.
5. INGREDIENT TIP: Packaged nutritional yeast can be found in the baking aisle of most grocery stores, and in the bulk section of health stores.
6. INGREDIENT TIP: Did you know butternut squash is technically a fruit? It's true, and it's because the squash contains seeds. It is also low in fat, high in fiber, and provides some serious potassium and vitamin B6!

Nutritional Facts Per Serving:
- Calories: 520;
- Total fat: 14g;
- Saturated fat: 2g;
- Sodium: 654mg;
- Carbs: 78g;
- Fiber: 10g;
- Protein: 23g

Sweet Potato & Black Bean Tacos

Serves: 4 TO 6

Ingredients:
- 1 to 2 tablespoons olive oil
- ½ sweet onion, diced
- 1 large sweet potato, diced
- 1 red bell pepper, diced
- 1 garlic clove, minced
- 1 tomato, diced
- 1 (15-ounce) can black beans, rinsed and drained
- 1 canned chipotle pepper in adobo sauce, diced
- 1 to 2 teaspoons adobo sauce from the can
- 1 to 2 teaspoons chili powder
- ½ teaspoon salt
- ½ teaspoon ground cumin
- ½ cup DIY Vegetable Stock, or store-bought stock
- 1 tablespoon freshly squeezed lime juice
- Zest of 1 lime
- Corn or flour tortillas, for serving
- 1 avocado, peeled, pitted, and mashed
- ¼ cup fresh cilantro, chopped
- Cashew Sour Cream, for serving (optional)
- Garden Salsa, for serving (optional)
- Sliced jalapeño peppers, for serving (optional)
- Sliced red cabbage, for serving (optional)

Directions:
1. On your Instant Pot®, select Sauté Low. When the display reads "Hot," add the oil and heat until it shimmers. Add the onion. Cook for 1 minute, stirring. Add the sweet potato and bell pepper. Cook for 1 minute, stirring so nothing burns. Turn off the Instant Pot® and add the garlic. Cook for 30 seconds to 1 minute, stirring.
2. Add the tomato, black beans, chipotle, adobo sauce, chili powder, salt, cumin, stock, and lime juice. Lock the lid and turn the steam release handle to Sealing. Using the Manual function, set the cooker to High Pressure for 4 minutes (3 minutes at sea level).
3. When the cook time is complete, turn off the Instant Pot® and let the pressure release naturally for 5 minutes; quick release any remaining pressure.
4. Carefully remove the lid. If there is too much liquid in the inner pot, select Sauté Low again and cook for 1 to 2 minutes, stirring constantly (it gets hot fast!).
5. Stir in the lime zest. Serve in the tortillas, topped with mashed avocado and cilantro and anything else your heart desires.
6. INGREDIENT TIP: Chipotle peppers in adobo are a common ingredient in Mexican dishes and can be found in the Mexican or ethnic aisle of most grocery stores. Most recipes call for a small amount, and you can freeze the remainder for another recipe.

Nutritional Facts Per Serving:
- Calories: 369;
- Total fat: 16g;
- Saturated fat: 2g;
- Sodium: 420mg;
- Carbs: 51g;
- Fiber: 15g;
- Protein: 12g

Chickpea Kale Korma

Serves: 4 TO 6

Ingredients:
- 1 cup dried chickpeas, rinsed
- 1 to 2 cups water
- ½ cup cashews, soaked in water overnight, drained and rinsed well
- 2 Roma tomatoes, quartered
- 3 garlic cloves, peeled
- ½-inch piece fresh ginger, peeled
- 1 (14-ounce) can lite coconut milk
- 1 teaspoon garam masala
- 1 teaspoon curry powder
- ½ to 1 teaspoon salt
- ½ teaspoon ground cumin
- ½ teaspoon ground coriander
- ½ teaspoon ground cardamom
- ½ teaspoon ground turmeric
- ½ teaspoon onion powder
- ¼ teaspoon freshly ground black pepper
- 1 bunch kale, leaves torn from stems and rinsed
- Hot cooked rice, for serving (optional)

Directions:
1. In your Instant Pot®, combine the chickpeas and enough water to cover. Lock the lid and turn the steam release handle to Sealing. Using the Manual function, set the cooker to High Pressure for 45 minutes (38 minutes at sea level).
2. When the cook time is complete, let the pressure release naturally for 15 minutes; quick release any remaining pressure.
3. Carefully remove the lid. Drain the chickpeas and return them to the Instant Pot®.
4. In a high-speed blender or food processor, combine the cashews, tomatoes, garlic, and ginger. Blend until smooth. Add the coconut milk and pulse a few more times to combine. Add this purée to the chickpeas along with the garam masala, curry powder, salt, cumin, coriander, cardamom, turmeric, onion powder, pepper, and kale.
5. On your Instant Pot®, select Sauté Low. Simmer for 8 to 10 minutes until the kale and beans have absorbed the flavor. Serve with rice, if desired.
6. SUBSTITUTION TIP: Kale is my go-to, but you can easily substitute spinach, collard greens, Swiss chard, or any other greens you have on hand.

Nutritional Facts Per Serving:
- Calories: 442;
- Total fat: 21g;
- Saturated fat: 10g;
- Sodium: 377mg;
- Carbs: 52g;
- Fiber: 11g;
- Protein: 18g

Deconstructed Cabbage Rolls

Serves: 6 TO 8

Ingredients:

For the tempeh
- 1 tablespoon olive oil
- 1 (8-ounce) package unflavored tempeh, crumbled
- 2 teaspoons Montreal steak seasoning

For the deconstructed cabbage rolls
- 1 cup basmati rice, rinsed and drained
- 1 cup water
- ½ teaspoon salt, plus more as needed
- 1½ cups DIY Vegetable Stock, or store-bought stock
- 1 head cabbage, thinly sliced
- 2 teaspoons vegan Worcestershire sauce
- 2 garlic cloves, minced
- 1 bay leaf
- ½ onion, diced
- 6 ounces tomato paste
- ½ teaspoon paprika
- ¼ teaspoon freshly ground black pepper, plus more as needed
- Pinch cayenne pepper, plus more as needed
- ¼ cup chopped fresh parsley

Directions:

1. In your Instant Pot®, combine the rice, water, and salt. Lock the lid and turn the steam release handle to Sealing. Using the Manual function, set the cooker to High Pressure for 8 minutes (7 minutes at sea level).
2. When the cook time is complete, let the pressure release naturally for 10 minutes; quick release any remaining pressure.
3. Carefully remove the lid and fluff the rice. Add the stock, cabbage, tomato paste, paprika, black pepper, and cayenne. Select Sauté Low again and cook for 4 to 5 minutes until the cabbage softens a little. Turn off the Instant Pot®, remove and discard the bay leaf, and stir in the parsley. Taste and season with more salt and pepper, as needed.

Nutritional Facts Per Serving:
- Calories: 276;
- Total fat: 7g;
- Saturated fat: 1g;
- Sodium: 455mg;
- Carbs: 43g;
- Fiber: 5g;
- Protein: 13g

Asian-Style Coconut Rice & Veggies

Serves: 4 TO 6

Ingredients:
- 1 cup jasmine rice, rinsed and drained
- 1 cup water
- 1 teaspoon salt
- ½ teaspoon ground ginger
- 1 tablespoon sesame oil
- 1 large carrot, sliced
- 1 small onion, diced
- 1 cup chopped bok choy
- 1 cup sugar snap peas, rinsed, tough ends removed
- 2 garlic cloves, minced
- 8 ounces white button mushrooms, sliced
- 1 (8-ounce) can sliced water chestnuts, drained
- 1 (14-ounce) can lite coconut milk
- 1 teaspoon Chinese five-spice
- 1 teaspoon soy sauce

Directions:
1. In your Instant Pot®, combine the rice, water, salt, and ginger. Lock the lid and turn the steam release handle to Sealing. Using the Manual function, set the cooker to High Pressure for 4 minutes (3 minutes at sea level).
2. When the cook time is complete, let the pressure release naturally for 5 minutes; quick release any remaining pressure.
3. Carefully remove the lid and fluff the rice. Transfer to a bowl and set aside.
4. On your Instant Pot®, select Sauté Low. When the display reads "Hot," add the oil and heat until it shimmers. Add the carrot, onion, bok choy, snap peas, garlic, mushrooms, and water chestnuts. Sauté for 2 to 3 minutes.
5. Stir in the coconut milk, five-spice powder, soy sauce, and cooked rice. Simmer for 5 to 6 minutes more, stirring occasionally, until the coconut milk is reduced.
6. INGREDIENT TIP: Frozen snap peas are great to keep in your freezer (I stock up when they're on sale!), but if you're using fresh peas, be sure to rinse them well and remove any thick or hard ends.

Nutritional Facts Per Serving:
- Calories: 418;
- Total fat: 13g;
- Saturated fat: 9g;
- Sodium: 738mg;
- Carbs: 70g;
- Fiber: 4g;
- Protein: 10g

Layered Mexican Casserole

Serves: 4 TO 6

Ingredients:
- Nonstick cooking spray, for preparing the springform pan
- 2 cups mashed sweet potatoes (about 2 potatoes)
- 1¼ cups Red Hot Enchilada Sauce, or 1 (10-ounce) can, divided
- 1 tablespoon freshly squeezed lime juice
- ½ to 1 teaspoon chili powder
- ½ teaspoon garlic powder
- ½ teaspoon onion powder
- 1 (15-ounce) can black beans, rinsed and drained
- 1 (10-ounce) can diced tomatoes with green chilies, drained
- ½ cup sliced scallion, green and light green parts, divided
- ¼ cup frozen sweet corn
- 8 or 9 taco-size, gluten-free corn tortillas
- Vegan cheese shreds, for topping (optional)
- ½ cup water
- Cashew Sour Cream, for serving
- Poblano Cheeze Sauce, for serving
- Sliced avocado, for serving

Directions:

1. Lightly coat the bottom and sides of a 7-inch springform pan with nonstick spray and set aside.
2. In a medium bowl, stir together the mashed sweet potatoes, 1 cup of enchilada sauce, the lime juice, chili powder, garlic powder, and onion powder.
3. In another medium bowl, stir together the black beans, tomatoes and green chilies, ¼ cup of scallion, the corn, and 3 tablespoons of enchilada sauce.
4. To build the casserole, spread the remaining 1 tablespoon of enchilada sauce on the bottom of the prepared pan. Add a layer of tortillas, torn as needed to get full coverage. Don't be afraid to overlap. Layer on one-third of the sweet potato mixture. Using a slotted spoon, top the sweet potato later with one-third of the black bean mixture. Repeat the tortilla layer, sweet potato layer, and black bean layer two more times. Top with the remaining ¼ cup of scallion. If using vegan cheese shreds, add them now.
5. Spray a piece of aluminum foil with nonstick spray and cover the pan tightly.
6. Pour the water into the Instant Pot® and place a trivet into the inner pot. Set the covered casserole on top of the trivet. Lock the lid and turn the steam release handle to Sealing. Using the Manual function, set the cooker to High Pressure for 8 minutes (7 minutes at sea level).
7. When the cook time is complete, let the pressure release naturally for 5 minutes; quick release any remaining pressure.
8. Carefully remove the lid and the trivet and casserole from the Instant Pot®. Set aside on a heat-resistant surface. Remove the foil and let cool for at least 5 minutes before releasing the sides of the pan. Plate and add desired toppings before serving.

Nutritional Facts Per Serving:
- Calories: 381;
- Total fat: 5g;
- Saturated fat: 1g;
- Sodium: 456mg;
- Carbs: 72g;
- Fiber: 16g;
- Protein: 15g

Moo Goo Gai Pan

Serves: 4 TO 6

Ingredients:

For the marinade
- 2 tablespoons DIY Vegetable Stock, or store-bought stock
- 2 tablespoons lite soy sauce
- 1 tablespoon sesame oil

For the stir-fry
- 1 (14-ounce) block firm tofu, pressed for least 1 hour, but overnight is best (the longer it's pressed, the more flavor it will soak up from the marinade), chopped into bite-size cubes
- 1 tablespoon sesame oil
- 8 ounces white mushrooms, sliced
- 1 cup sugar snap peas, rinsed, tough ends removed
- 1 carrot, sliced into matchsticks
- 1 garlic clove, minced
- 1-inch piece fresh ginger, peeled and grated
- 1 garlic clove, minced
- ½-inch piece fresh ginger, peeled and grated
- 1 cup DIY Vegetable Stock, or store-bought stock
- 2 tablespoons soy sauce
- 1 (8-ounce) can sliced water chestnuts, drained
- 1 (8-ounce) can bamboo shoots, drained
- 1 tablespoon cornstarch
- ⅓ cup water
- Hot cooked rice or noodles, for serving (optional)

Directions:

To make the marinade
1. In a small bowl, whisk the stock, soy sauce, oil, garlic, and ginger. Set aside.

To make the stir-fry

2. In a shallow dish, combine the tofu cubes and marinade. Cover the dish and let sit for at least 30 minutes. On your Instant Pot®, select Sauté Low. When the display reads "Hot," add the oil and heat until it shimmers. Add the marinated tofu. Cook for 8 to 10 minutes, using tongs to turn the tofu carefully.
3. Turn off the Instant Pot® and add the mushrooms, snap peas, carrot, garlic, ginger, stock, soy sauce, water chestnuts, and bamboo shoots. Using a large spoon, stir well. On your Instant Pot®, select Sauté Low again. Cover the pot with a tempered glass lid (either one you purchased for the Instant Pot® or another that fits) and simmer for 5 minutes, stirring occasionally.   In a small bowl, whisk the cornstarch and water. Add this slurry to the pot. Simmer, uncovered, for 5 minutes more, or until the sauce thickens. Serve over rice or noodles (if using).
4. TECHNIQUE TIP: I mentioned a few accessories for your Instant Pot® in chapter 1 (see here) and a tempered glass lid was one. It's very handy in recipes like this, when you need to keep an eye on what is cooking.

Nutritional Facts Per Serving:

Calories: 274;   Total fat: 12g;   Saturated fat: 2g;   Carbs: 33g;   Fiber: 4g;   Protein: 14g

Vegetable Lasagna

Serves: 4 TO 6

Ingredients:

For the tofu ricotta
- 1 (14-ounce) container firm tofu, pressed for 5 to 10 minutes
- ⅓ cup nutritional yeast
- 3 tablespoons nondairy milk, plus more as needed
- 2 teaspoons dried oregano
- 1½ teaspoons onion powder
- 1½ teaspoons garlic powder
- 1 teaspoon dried basil
- 1 teaspoon salt, plus more as needed
- Freshly ground black pepper
- For the lasagna
- Nonstick cooking spray, for preparing the springform pan
- 2 tablespoons plus 1 cup water, divided
- 1 small zucchini, diced (about 1 cup)
- ½ sweet onion, diced
- 1 garlic clove, minced
- ½ teaspoon salt
- Pinch red pepper flakes
- 6 to 8 dried lasagna noodles
- 4 cups butternut basil red sauce, or favorite red pasta sauce, divided
- 8 fresh basil leaves, chopped

Directions:

To make the tofu ricotta
1. In a large bowl, combine the tofu, nutritional yeast, milk, oregano, onion powder, garlic powder, basil, and salt, and season to taste with pepper. Using a wooden spoon or potato masher, break down the tofu and stir until everything is combined and the mixture is smooth. Stir in additional milk, by the tablespoon, if you need more moisture. Alternatively, combine the ingredients in a food processor and pulse a few times until smooth.

To make the lasagna

2. Lightly coat the bottom and sides of a 7-inch springform pan with nonstick spray. Set aside.
3. On your instant pot®, select sauté low. When the display reads "hot," Add 2 tablespoons of water to heat. Add the zucchini, onion, garlic, salt, and red pepper flakes. Cook for 2 to 3 minutes until they begin to soften. Turn off the instant pot® and remove the veggies.
4. Place a layer of lasagna noodles in the pot, breaking them to get maximum coverage. Spread 1 cup of sauce over the noodles and top with half the veggie mix and half the ricotta. Repeat. Finally, add a third layer of lasagna noodles and another 1 cup of sauce. (you should have 1 cup left.) lightly coat a piece of aluminum foil with nonstick spray and tightly cover the pan.
5. Pour 1 cup of water into the instant pot® and place a trivet into the inner pot. Set the covered lasagna on top of the trivet. Lock the lid and turn the steam release handle to sealing. Using the manual function, set the cooker to high pressure for 25 minutes (21 minutes at sea level).
6. When the cook time is complete, let the pressure release naturally for 15 minutes; quick release any remaining pressure.
7. Carefully remove the lid and the trivet and pan from the instant pot® and remove the foil. Let the lasagna cool for at least 5 minutes before releasing the sides of the pan (it helps to leave it on the trivet during this time). The longer you wait to release, the easier it will be to slice.
8. Top with fresh basil and the remaining sauce.
9. TECHNIQUE TIP: I use a full batch of tofu ricotta in my lasagna because I like it a little gooey and messy. If you're using vegan cheese in yours (or if you just want a super neat lasagna), scale back and only use half to three-fourths of the ricotta.

Nutritional Facts Per Serving:
- Calories: 414;
- Total fat: 8g;
- Saturated fat: 1g;
- Sodium: 1239mg;
- Carbs: 64g;
- Fiber: 12g;
- Protein: 32g

TREATS, SWEETS & DESSERTS

Bourbon Apple Crisp

Serves: 4

Ingredients:
- 5 apples, peeled and cut into thick slices
- 2 tablespoons maple syrup
- 2 tablespoons ground cinnamon
- ½ teaspoon ground nutmeg
- Salt
- ¼ cup water
- ¼ cup bourbon
- 4 tablespoons vegan butter
- ¾ cup old-fashioned oats
- ¼ cup all-purpose flour
- ½ cup packed light brown sugar

Directions:
1. In your Instant Pot®, stir together the apples, maple syrup, cinnamon, nutmeg, and pinch of salt. Cover the apples with the water and bourbon.
2. In a medium microwave-safe bowl, microwave the butter until just barely melted. Add the oats, flour, brown sugar, and ½ teaspoon of salt. Stir to combine. Spoon the oat mixture over the apples, getting as much coverage as possible. Lock the lid and turn the steam release handle to Sealing. Using the Manual function, set the cooker to High Pressure for 8 minutes (7 minutes at sea level).
3. When the cook time is complete, let the pressure release naturally for 10 to 12 minutes; quick release any remaining pressure. Turn off the Instant Pot®.
4. Carefully remove the lid and let the crisp rest for a few minutes to thicken before serving.
5. INGREDIENT TIP: If you don't want to use bourbon, simply add another ¼ cup of water.

Nutritional Facts Per Serving:
- Calories: 476;
- Total fat: 13g;
- Saturated fat: 2g;
- Sodium: 184mg;
- Carbs: 86g;
- Fiber: 10g;
- Protein: 3g

Vanilla Poached Pears With Caramel Sauce

Serves: 4

Ingredients:
- 3 cups water
- 2 cups white wine
- 2 cups sugar
- 1 whole vanilla bean, split and scraped
- 1 cinnamon stick
- 4 Bosc pears, ripe but not soft
- 1 lemon, halved
- 1 batch Easy Caramel Sauce, warmed

Directions:
1. On your Instant Pot®, select Sauté Low. When the display reads "Hot," add the water, white wine, sugar, vanilla bean and seeds, and cinnamon stick, stirring well. Cook for 1 to 2 minutes, or until the sugar dissolves completely. Cancel Sauté and select Keep Warm.
2. Gently peel the pears. If presentation is important, keep the stems intact. Rub the pears with the lemon halves to prevent browning and add the pears to the Instant Pot®. Lock the lid and turn the steam release handle to Sealing. Using the Manual function, set the cooker to High Pressure for 3 minutes.
3. When the cook time is complete, quick release the pressure.
4. Carefully remove the lid and remove the pears. Set aside to cool. Save the sauce and pour it over the pears once cooled. Serve, warm or at room temperature, topped with caramel sauce.

Nutritional Facts Per Serving:
- Calories: 520;
- Total fat: 9g;
- Saturated fat: 9g;
- Sodium: 60mg;
- Carbs: 107g;
- Fiber: 7g;
- Protein: 1g

Fresh Fruit Compote

Serves: makes 4 cups

Ingredients:
- 6 cups mixed berries (I like a 2:1 ratio of strawberries to blueberries)
- 1½ cups sugar
- ¼ cup freshly squeezed orange juice

Directions:
1. In your Instant Pot®, combine the berries, sugar, and orange juice. Lock the lid and turn the steam release handle to Sealing. Using the Manual function, set the cooker to High Pressure for 3 minutes.
2. When the cook time is complete, turn off the Instant Pot® and let the pressure release naturally for 10 minutes; quick release any remaining pressure.
3. Carefully remove the lid. Select Sauté Medium. Stir the berry mixture and cook for 5 to 10 minutes (depending on how much liquid there is) so some of the excess liquid evaporates. Switch to Low if it's spattering too much. When you've reached the desired consistency, let the compote cool a bit before enjoying.

Nutritional Facts Per Serving: (½ CUP):
- Calories: 179;
- Total fat: 0g;
- Saturated fat: 0g;
- Sodium: 0mg;
- Carbs: 47g;
- Fiber: 2g;
- Protein: 1g

Cinnamon-Vanilla Applesauce

Serves: 6 TO 8

Ingredients:
- 3 pounds apples, cored and quartered, no need to peel
- ⅓ cup water
- 1 teaspoon vanilla extract
- 1 teaspoon ground cinnamon, plus more as needed
- 1 teaspoon freshly squeezed lemon juice
- ½ teaspoon salt

Directions:
1. In your Instant Pot®, combine the apples, water, vanilla, cinnamon, lemon juice, and salt. Lock the lid and turn the steam release handle to Sealing. Using the Manual function, set the cooker to High Pressure for 5 minutes (4 minutes at sea level).
2. When the cook time is complete, let the pressure release naturally for 10 minutes; quick release any remaining pressure.
3. Carefully remove the lid. Using an immersion blender, blend the applesauce until smooth. Taste and add more cinnamon, as desired.
4. FREEZER TIP: Pack into freezer-safe food storage bags for when you need a snack. Just thaw in your refrigerator. Applesauce also works well as an egg substitute for baking, so it's versatile to keep on hand.

Nutritional Facts Per Serving:
- Calories: 61;
- Total fat: 0g;
- Saturated fat: 0g;
- Sodium: 195mg;
- Carbs: 13g;
- Fiber: 3g;
- Protein: 0g

Bourbon Apple Crisp

Serves: 4

Ingredients:
- Apples – 5, peeled and chopped
- Maple syrup – 2 Tbsp.
- Ground cinnamon – 2 Tbsp.
- Ground nutmeg – ½ tsp.
- Salt
- Water – ¼ cup
- Bourbon – ¼ cup or more water
- Vegan butter – 4 Tbsp.
- Old-fashioned oats – ¾ cups
- All-purpose flour – ¼ cup
- Light brown sugar – ½ cup

Directions:
1. In the Instant Pot, stir together the maple syrup, apples, cinnamon, nutmeg, and a pinch of salt. Cover the apples with bourbon and water.
2. In a bowl, microwave the butter until just barely melted.
3. Add ½ tsp. salt, brown sugar, flour, and oats. Mix.
4. Spoon the oat mixture over the apples.
5. Cover the Instant Pot.
6. Cook on High for 7 minutes.
7. Do a natural release and open.
8. Serve.

Nutritional Facts Per Serving:
- Calories: 476
- Fat: 13g
- Carb: 86g
- Protein: 3g

Poached Pears With Caramel Sauce

Serves: 4

Ingredients:
- Water – 3 cups
- White wine – 2 cups
- Sugar – 2 cups
- Whole vanilla bean – 1, split and scraped
- Cinnamon – 1 stick
- Ripe but not soft pears – 4
- Lemon – 1 halved
- Caramel sauce – ½ cup, warmed

Directions:
1. Press Sauté and add white wine, water, sugar, vanilla beans, seeds, and cinnamon stick. Mix well.
2. Cook for 2 minutes.
3. Press Cancel.
4. Peel the pears and rub with lemon halves then add to the Instant Pot.
5. Cover the Instant Pot.
6. Cook on High for 3 minutes.
7. Do a quick release.
8. Open and remove the pears.
9. Cool and save the sauce.
10. Pour the pot sauce over the pears, topped with caramel sauce.

Nutritional Facts Per Serving:
- Calories: 520
- Fat: 9g
- Carb: 107g
- Protein: 1g

Fresh Fruit Compote

Serves: 4

Ingredients:
- Mixed berries – 6 cups
- Sugar – 1 ½ cups
- Orange juice – ¼ cup

Directions:
1. In the Instant Pot, combine the orange juice, sugar, and berries.
2. Cover the Instant Pot
3. Cook on High for 3 minutes.
4. Do a natural release.
5. Open the lid and press Sauté.
6. Stir-fry for 5 to 10 minutes to evaporate the liquid.
7. Stop cooking when thickened.
8. Cool and serve.

Nutritional Facts Per Serving:
- Calories: 179
- Fat: 0g
- Carb: 47g
- Protein: 1g

Cinnamon Coconut Rice Pudding

Serves: 4

Ingredients:
- Jasmin rice – 1 cup, rinsed and drained
- Full-fat coconut milk – 1 (14-ounce) can
- Water – 2 cups
- Ground cinnamon – 2 tsp.
- Vanilla extract – 1 ½ tsp.
- Ground nutmeg – ½ tsp.
- Salt – 1 tsp.
- Sugar – ¼ cup
- Nondairy milk to thin after cooking
- Maple syrup, coconut flakes, and raisins for topping

Directions:
1. In the Instant Pot, combine the sugar, salt, nutmeg, vanilla, cinnamon, water, coconut milk, and rice.
2. Cover and cook on High for 17 minutes.
3. Do a natural release.
4. Remove the lid and add milk to thicken the pudding.
5. Serve.

Nutritional Facts Per Serving:
- Calories: 504
- Fat: 29g
- Carb: 57g
- Protein: 6g

Sticky Rice & Fresh Fruit

Serves: 4

Ingredients:
- Full-fat coconut milk – 1 cup
- Sugar – ¼ cup
- Salt – ½ tsp.
- Water – 2 ½ cups, divided
- Sweet rice – 1 cup, rinsed and drained
- Sliced fresh fruit for serving

Directions:
1. Combine the coconut milk, sugar, and salt in a saucepan and heat over low heat.
2. Cook and stir for 3 minutes, don't boil. Remove from the heat.
3. Pour 1 cup water into the Instant Pot. Place a trivet.
4. In a bowl combine the remaining 1 ¼ cups water and the rice. Make sure the rice is cover with the water.
5. On top of the trivet, place the bowl.
6. Cover the Instant Pot.
7. Cook on High for 12 minutes.
8. Do a natural release.
9. Open and add half the coconut sauce.
10. Cover.
11. Allow to let sit for 5 minutes, so the rice absorbs the liquid.
12. Top each serving with fruit and additional coconut sauce.

Nutritional Facts Per Serving:
- Calories: 230
- Fat: 14g
- Carb: 26g
- Protein: 2g

Cherry Pie

Serves: 6

Ingredients:
- Cherries – 2 pounds, pitted
- Pinch salt
- Brandy – 1/3 cup
- Juice of ½ lime
- Sugar – 2/3 cup
- Cornstarch – 3 Tbsp.
- Mini Fillo shells for serving

Directions:
1. In a bowl combine the brandy and cherries. Soak for 30 minutes, stirring occasionally.
2. Press Sauté on the Instant Pot.
3. Pour the cherries and the liquid. Stir in cornstarch, sugar, salt, and lime juice.
4. Stir-fry for 10 to 15 minutes.
5. Cool for a few minutes, then spoon the filling into the Fillo shells.

Nutritional Facts Per Serving:
- Calories: 288
- Fat: 3g
- Carb: 61g
- Protein: 4g

Mango Coconut Rice Pudding

Serves: 4

Ingredients:
- Arborio rice – ¾ cup
- Coconut milk – 1 can
- Brown sugar – ½ cup
- Mango – peeled and cubed for garnishing
- Chopped almonds and shredded coconut for garnishing
- Vanilla essence - 1 tsp.
- Water – 2 cups
- Salt – 1 tsp.

Directions:
1. In the Instant Pot, add the rice, coconut milk, salt, water, and sugar and mix.
2. Cover the Instant Pot. Cook on High for 7 minutes.
3. Remove and cool. Serve with garnishing on top.

Nutritional Facts Per Serving:
- Calories: 439
- Fat: 19.5g
- Carb: 63.6g
- Protein: 6g

Tapioca Pudding

Serves: 4

Ingredients:
- Tapioca pearls – ½ cup
- Coconut milk – 1 ½ cups
- Splash of vanilla
- Full fat coconut cream – 1 small cream
- Agave nectar – 1/3 cup

Directions:
1. Pour int 2 cups water to the Instant Pot   Place a trivet.
2. Combine allin a bowl and place the bowl on top of the trivet.
3. Cover the Instant Pot.   Cook on High for 7 minutes.
4. Do a natural release.   Open and serve.

Nutritional Facts Per Serving:
- Calories: 424
- Fat: 42.9g
- Carb: 12.3g
- Protein: 5g

APPETIZERS, STARTERS & SIDES

Cowboy Caviar

Serves: 3

Ingredients:

Caviar
- Dry black beans – ¾ cup, rinsed, drained
- Fresh or frozen corn – 1 ½ cups
- Fresh tomatoes – 1 cup, diced
- Red pepper – ½, chopped
- Red onion – ¼ cup, chopped
- Cilantro – 2 tbsp. chopped

Sauce
- Mexican tomato sauce – 1 can (22g)
- Salt – ½ tsp.
- Chili powder – 2 tsp.
- Brown sugar – 2 tsp.
- Rice vinegar – 1 tbsp.
- Juice of ½ lime

Directions:
1. Place the beans in the instant pot, add 3 cups of water and cover with the lid.
2. Cook 25 minutes on High. Then do a natural release.
3. Mix all the sauce .
4. In a separate bowl.
5. Place the beans in a bowl. Add the remainingin there and pour the sauce over the bowl of caviar .
6. Stir and serve.

Nutritional Facts Per Serving:
- Calories: 263
- Fat: 2.1g
- Carb: 50.8g
- Protein: 14.1g

Beans With Jalapenos

Serves: 3

Ingredients:
- Dry pinto beans – 1 ½ cups, rinsed
- Chili powder – 1 tbsp.
- Cumin – 1 tbsp.
- Salt – 1 tsp.
- Salsa – ¾ cups
- Diced jalapenos – 4 oz.

Directions:
1. Place the beans in the Instant Pot. Add enough water, so the beans are submerged by 2-inch water.
2. Cook on High for 45 minutes, then do a natural release.
3. Place the drained beans in a bowl. Add salt, cumin and chili powder.
4. With a hand mixture, blend until it reaches your desired consistency.
5. Add diced jalapenos and salsa to the beans and mix well.
6. Serve with tortilla chips.

Nutritional Facts Per Serving:
- Calories: 61
- Fat: 1.3g
- Carb: 12.5g
- Protein: 3.2g

Candid Carrots

Serves: 4

Ingredients:
- Baby carrots – 1 pound
- Water – 1 cup
- Vegan butter – 3 Tbsp.
- Light brown sugar – 3 Tbsp.
- Salt – ½ tsp.

Directions:
1. Pour in water into the Instant Pot, then place a steamer basket. Add the carrots on top. Close and cook on High for 2 minutes.
2. Do a quick release. Open and add the butter. Let it melt for 1 minute.
3. Add the salt, and brown sugar and mix to coat. Serve.

Nutritional Facts Per Serving:
- Calories: 123
- Fat: 7g
- Carb: 16g
- Protein: 1g

Lemon Ginger Asparagus

Serves: 4

Ingredients:
- Asparagus – 1 bunch, tough ends removed
- Water – 1 cup
- Olive oil – 2 Tbsp.
- Lemon juice – 1 Tbsp.
- Salt – ½ to 1 tsp.
- Grated peeled fresh ginger – ½ tsp.

Directions:
1. Add water to the Instant Pot. Place a steamer basket into the Instant Pot and add asparagus on top.
2. Close and cook for 0 minutes.
3. Do a quick release.
4. In a bowl, stir together ginger, salt, lemon juice, and oil.
5. Add the asparagus to the bowl.
6. Toss and serve.

Nutritional Facts Per Serving:
- Calories: 84
- Fat: 7g
- Carb: 5g
- Protein: 3g

Steamed Artichokes

Serves: 2

Ingredients:
- Artichokes – 4, rinsed, and prepared
- Lemon – 1 large, cut into ¼ inch thick round slices
- Water – 1 cup
- Garlic – 2 cloves, peeled

Directions:
1. Rub the lemon wedges over the entire outside of the artichokes. This adds extra flavor and prevents browning.
2. In the Instant Pot, add garlic, lemon slices, and water.
3. In the Instant Pot, place a trivet, and add artichokes on top, stem-side down.
4. Cover and cook on High for 9 minutes.
5. Do a quick release and serve.

Nutritional Facts Per Serving:
- Calories: 165
- Fat: 1g
- Carb: 38g
- Protein: 11g

Candied Carrots

Serves: 4 TO 6

Ingredients:
- 1 (1-pound) bag baby carrots
- 1 cup water
- 3 tablespoons vegan butter
- 3 tablespoons packed light brown sugar
- ½ to 1 teaspoon salt

Directions:
1. Put the carrots in a steamer basket and place the basket into the Instant Pot®. Pour in the water. Lock the lid and turn the steam release handle to Sealing. Using the Manual function, set the cooker to High Pressure for 2 minutes.
2. When the cook time is complete, quick release the pressure.
3. Carefully remove the lid and add the butter, letting it melt into the carrots for 1 minute or so.
4. Add the brown sugar and salt. Stir, stir, stir until the carrots are coated. Taste and add a touch more salt, if you'd like.
5. INGREDIENT TIP: Both light and dark brown sugars are made with sugar and molasses. Dark brown sugar has more molasses and, therefore, a stronger flavor. I tend to use light brown sugar, but both are delicious and can be substituted for each other.

Nutritional Facts Per Serving:
- Calories: 123;
- Total fat: 7g;
- Saturated fat: 1g;
- Sodium: 354mg;
- Carbs: 16g;
- Fiber: 3g;
- Protein: 1g

Anything-But-Basic Baked Potatoes

Serves: 4

Ingredients:
- 4 medium russet potatoes, scrubbed well, pierced on all sides with a fork
- 1 cup water
- Toppings, as desired

Directions:
1. Add the water and a trivet to the Instant Pot®. Place the potatoes on the trivet. Lock the lid and turn the steam release handle to Sealing. Using the Manual function, set the cooker to High Pressure for 15 minutes (13 minutes at sea level).
2. When the cook time is complete, let the Instant Pot® go into Keep Warm mode and let the pressure release naturally for 15 minutes; quick release any remaining pressure.
3. Add toppings and ta-da!

Nutritional Facts Per Serving:
- Calories: 147;
- Total fat: 0g;
- Saturated fat: 0g;
- Sodium: 13mg;
- Carbs: 34g;
- Fiber: 5g;
- Protein: 4g

Lemon Ginger Asparagus

Serves: 4 TO 6

Ingredients:
- 1 bunch asparagus, tough ends removed, halved if remaining pieces are longer than 4 inches
- 1 cup water
- 2 tablespoons olive oil
- 1½ teaspoons to 1 tablespoon freshly squeezed lemon juice
- ½ to 1 teaspoon salt
- ½ to ¾ teaspoon grated peeled fresh ginger

Directions:
1. Place the asparagus in a steamer basket and put the basket into the Instant Pot®. Add the water. Lock the lid and turn the steam release handle to Sealing. Using the Manual function, set the cooker to Low Pressure for 0 minutes.
2. When the cook time is complete, quick release the pressure.
3. In a serving bowl, stir together the oil, lemon juice, ½ teaspoon of salt, and ½ teaspoon of ginger.
4. Carefully remove the lid and add the asparagus to the bowl. Toss to combine. Taste and add the remaining lemon juice and/or ginger, as needed.

Nutritional Facts Per Serving:
- Calories: 84;
- Total fat: 7g;
- Saturated fat: 1g;
- Sodium: 294mg;
- Carbs: 5g;
- Fiber: 2g;
- Protein: 3g

"Roasted" Garlic

Serves: 4

Ingredients:
- 1 cup water
- 4 large heads garlic, tops cut off to expose just the top of each clove
- Olive oil (I recommend butter-infused)
- Crusty bread, for serving

Directions:
1. Add the water and a trivet to the Instant Pot®. Place the garlic on the trivet, cut-side up. Lock the lid and turn the steam release handle to Sealing. Using the Manual function, set the cooker to High Pressure for 6 minutes (5 minutes at sea level).
2. When the cook time is complete, turn off the cooker and let the pressure release naturally until the pin drops, about 10 minutes.
3. Carefully remove the lid. Using tongs, transfer the garlic to a baking sheet or other heatproof dish. Generously drizzle with olive oil, making sure all the garlic gets oiled! Broil on low for about 5 minutes. Watch so it doesn't burn, but you want it to be golden and caramelized. Remove from the oven and let cool for at least 10 minutes.
4. Serve immediately, plated in the skins as is (that's how it's done in restaurants). Your guests can use their butter knives to scoop out the cloves for schmearing.

Nutritional Facts Per Serving:
- Calories: 408;
- Total fat: 26g;
- Saturated fat: 4g;
- Sodium: 318mg;
- Carbs: 39g;
- Fiber: 2g;
- Protein: 8g

Steamed Artichokes

Serves: 2 TO 4

Ingredients:
- 4 or 5 artichokes, rinsed
- 1 large lemon
- 1 cup water
- 2 garlic cloves, peeled

Directions:
1. With a sharp knife, cut about 1 inch off the top (petal end) of one artichoke. Remove the tough outer leaves (usually one or two layers), and trim off the stem. Repeat with the remaining artichokes.
2. Cut most of the lemon into ¼-inch-thick round slices, leaving one end. Cut that end into wedges. Rub the lemon wedges over the entire outside of the artichokes, focusing on the cut edges. This keeps them from browning and adds extra flavor.
3. In your Instant Pot®, combine the water, lemon slices, and garlic. Place a trivet into the pot and put the artichokes on the trivet in a single layer, stem-side down. Lock the lid and turn the steam release handle to Sealing. Using the Manual function, set the cooker to High Pressure for 10 minutes (9 minutes at sea level).
4. When the cook time is complete, quick release the pressure.
5. Carefully remove the lid. Using tongs, remove the artichokes and serve warm. Enjoy by dipping each leaf in your favorite dipping sauce and pulling out the artichoke meat with your teeth.
6. SERVING TIP: Artichokes are delicious on their own, but let's be real— the dip matters! You can change it up according to your mood or the season, but my go-to is champagne vinaigrette. Try salad dressing or even the Poblano Cheeze Sauce!

Nutritional Facts Per Serving:
Calories: 165; Total fat: 1g; Saturated fat: 0g; Sodium: 306mg; Carbs: 38g; Fiber: 18g; Protein: 11g

Milton Keynes UK
Ingram Content Group UK Ltd.
UKHW020404150324
439439UK00009B/1184